W9-AKC-918

"Inspiring stories capturing the passion of the tenacious entrepreneurs who make up the soul of our immigrant-nation's entrepreneurial spirit."

—John Stavig, Director, Gary S. Holmes Center for Entrepreneurship, Carlson School of Management, University of Minnesota

"*Green Card Entrepreneur Voices* is a fascinating account that captures an intimate portrait of immigrants, their journeys and their perseverance to create successful businesses in Minnesota. This is an important piece of work that breathes new life into the often overlooked story of how immigrants benefit America."

—Ibrahim Hirsi, staff writer at MinnPost

"Stories inform, inspire, and illuminate possibilities. *Green Card Entrepreneur Voices* introduces us to people who have started businesses - people who happen to be immigrants. Through this beautiful collection, we get to meet these individuals and hear their engaging stories."

—Ann Rupnow, UW-Eau Claire Entrepreneurship Program

"*Green Card Entrepreneur Voices* is an invitation from Minnesota immigrants into their unique, personal, and courageous journeys. Drawing on their imaginative and inspiring stories the book masterfully weaves metaphors, visions, hopes, and struggles in a colorful and creative way. With sensibility and profound honesty, their stories help us connect and expand our human capacity to love. Given the social challenges of our times, *Green Card Entrepreneur Voices* is a must read for those seeking to transcend the intelligence of the heart and the mind."

—Dr. Ramon A. Pastrano IV, CEO-President ImpactLives Inc.

"I was moved by these heartfelt essays. They demonstrate the courage, resilience and tenacity of this group of entrepreneurs. It is clear from the stories what an asset immigrants are to this country. They contribute to the economy and make America a richer, more interesting, and stronger country."

—Joanna Ramirez Barrett, Ph.D.. Vice President of Business Solutions, MEDA

"What is it like to leave your home country to go to America? What do new arrivals do to earn money after coming to the US? These are questions I hear many ask about those new to America. This book answers those questions and tells how individuals transitioned from entry-level jobs to running their own enterprises. In their own words,these immigrants share their personal stories in a way that is open, honest and inspiring."

—Terri Barreiro, Author of *Social Entrepreneurship: From Issue to Viable Plan*; Co-founder of Impact Hub MSP; Adjunct Professor, Humphrey School of Public Affairs, University of Minnesota

"*Green Card Entrepreneur Voices* gives us a glimpse into the hearts and minds of the fastest growing segment of entrepreneurialism in our region. The stories are captivating and inspired. It's a must read!"

—Jonathan Weinhagen, President & CEO, The Minneapolis Regional Chamber of Commerce

"At the breakneck speed we live our days, we may notice the immigrants all around us, but we don't stop often enough to connect and learn their stories—their struggles and triumphs. *Green Card Entrepreneur Voices* allows each reader to slow down and take the time to hear and see the stories of immigrants come to life off the page—allowing us to look beyond ourselves and understand the importance of immigrants and the entrepreneurial spirit and hard work throughout the generations. Read it today and then share it again and again with friends and family."

—Kathleen M. Lohmar Exel, Foundation Director of the Saint Paul Area Chamber of Commerce and a Former Immigration Attorney

Green Card Entrepreneur Voices

How-To Business Stories from Minnesota Immigrants

Tashitaa Tufaa, Bo Thao-Urabe, Dario Mejia, Hassan Syed,
Veronica Quillien, Vikas Narula, Tomme Beevas, Batul Walji,
Amara Kamara, Ruhel Islam, Mary Anne & Sergio Quiroz,
Caterina Cerano, Trung Pham, Marcia Malzahn, Haji Yusuf,
Andrés A. Parra, Ameeta Jaiswal-Dale, Wanny Huynh, José Figueroa

Authors

Tea Rozman Clark, Rachel Mueller
Editors

ISBN 13: 978-0-9974960-7-9
LCCN: 2018942670

Printed in the United States of America
First Printing: 2018
20 19 18 17 16   5 4 3 2 1

Edited by Tea Rozman Clark, Rachel Mueller

Cover design by Nupoor Gordon
Cover illustration by rawpixel.com/shutterstock
Interior design by José Guzmán

Photography, videography by Media Active: Youth Produced Media

Wise Ink Creative Publishing
837 Glenwood Ave.
Minneapolis, MN 55405
www.wiseinkpub.com

We dedicate this book to all the people who have believed in, mentored, worked alongside, and lifted up immigrant and refugee entrepreneurs, supporting them to reach their fullest potential.

Table of Contents

Foreword	i
Acknowledgments	v
Introduction	ix
How to Use this Book	xv
World Map	xvi
Personal Essays	xix
Tashitaa Tufaa—Ethiopia	1
Bo Thao-Urabe—Laos	7
Dario Mejia—Ecuador	15
Hassan Syed—Pakistan	23
Veronica Quillien—Cameroon	31
Vikas Narula—Canada	39
Tomme Beevas—Jamaica	45
Batul Walji—Democratic Republic of the Congo	51
Amara Kamara—Liberia	55
Ruhel Islam—Bangladesh	67
Mary Anne & Sergio Quiroz—The Philippines/Mexico	73
Caterina Cerano—Italy	83
Trung Pham—Vietnam	89
Marcia Malzahn—Nicaragua	95
Haji Yusuf—Kenya (Somali)	105
Andrés A. Parra—Venezuela	113
Ameeta Jaiswal-Dale—India	121
Wanny Huynh—Vietnam	129
José Figueroa—Puerto Rico	137
Afterword	147
Glossary	149
About the Advisory Team	152
About Green Card Voices	153

Foreword

My entrepreneurial journey began when I was a young boy, when I told my father that I did not want to follow in his footsteps to become a civil service officer. Many generations, on both sides of my family, had served as senior civil servants during the British Raj; my father was the second officer in all of India commissioned after it became newly independent. Being a good student, I would have very likely qualified for such a prestigious profession as well. My mother's advice was, as it had often been since childhood, "You will do what settles down in your own mind."

A business profession was also out—businessmen, as depicted in popular cinema, were crooks and bloodsuckers and were to be despised. A newly established engineering program seemed promising, but after the final exam and before the final submission of my thesis, I recall sitting with a few classmates on a hot May night, crying that I had made a colossal mistake—I had no interest in engineering!

A steel foundry job quickly led me to the position of production control officer. Driven to improve the processes at the foundry, I came across the newly emerging field of operations research. Exchanging correspondence with some practitioners in the field led to them encouraging me to join a formal program.

I was about to be married, and my fiancée was working on her own degree in linguistics. Both of us scrambled to apply for our respective disciplines at various universities. My best bet was Stanford, hers Columbia. When we looked up the map of the US, it was clear that this was not going to work—thus, we picked the University of Minnesota as our middle ground. We planned to move somewhere else after we finished our studies, but here we are after nearly fifty years.

I was the first graduate with an MS in operations research (OR) from the University of Minnesota. Since my objective was to apply these techniques to business and industry, I felt it important to formally study them by enrolling in an MBA program. Being a newly minted OR person, I got the opportunity to teach an independent class in production management, which, through a connection with one of my students, led to a fifteen-year position at a leading company in the car rental industry.

When the company was sold, I used my severance pay to contemplate my next steps. What stood out was the fact that we had succeeded against stiff competition by doing many innovative things—I wanted to study more of how that could be harnessed. Who innovates against all odds? An entrepreneur. I had finally arrived at my raison d'être.

Fast-forward. I went back to school to write my PhD dissertation on entrepreneurism, which formed the basis of the very first university program in entrepreneurship in my region, and became a tenured professor. After ten years, I left academia to start a few companies. The last one was sold in 2013. Now I run the Institute for Innovators and Entrepreneurs, a nonprofit organization that advocates for entrepreneurs in the state of Minnesota.

Entrepreneurs have to constantly reconcile emerging norms with their previously held internal beliefs. We see the normalization of the myth that America is always a land of opportunity despite the hardships immigrants all too often encounter. The resolution of such tensions is a skill that can lead to unimagined destinations.

The stories in *Green Card Entrepreneur Voices* are so important because they enumerate all the divergent paths people have taken to settle in their new home. Some came here as refugees due to treachery of war; others were driven by personal circumstances to find a better life; still others simply sought opportunities. All of them describe the series of coincidences and intuitive assumptions that, like mine, seemed random until hindsight locked them into a pattern. We all have a story inside of us which is much more interesting than what appears on the surface. Our words may be different, but there is a continuity underneath them all.

Green Card Voices' storytelling approach immediately resonated with me because it resembled lightly processed case studies in a university setting. The case method is a proven educational tool that presents a situation complete with challenges, constraints, and incomplete information. It forces the reader into the role of the decision maker and helps them analyze their own issues, exercise judgment, and make decisions.

The Achieving Society, a book by David McClelland, drew evidence from history and some forty contemporary nations to show how one human motive is a precursor to periods of entrepreneurship and rapid economic growth: the need for Achievement (nAchievement), a desire to excel for its own sake. Communities that share folk tales and stories—especially those describing success after overcoming adversity—are powerful sources of enstilling the drive of 'nAchievement' in their societies. The future economic prosperity of a society depends on such stories we tell the next generation. This particular volume is the latest collection of those who chose the path of becoming an entrepreneur in Minnesota.

Immigrants have a long history of starting businesses in the United States. From Alexander Graham Bell to Sergey Brin, immigrants have created some of America's most iconic companies. Their stories are broadly available. Through this book, we now have a deeper view, previously unavailable, into Minnesotan companies such as **Panache**, which has spiced up apple cider and several other beverages; **Curio Dance,** which has brought a Julliard-educated teacher to Stillwater; **Gandhi Mahal Restaurant**, an aquaponics restaurant in Minneapolis; **Metropolitan Transportation Network**, the provider of more than three hundred school buses; **Star Banners**, which made the advertising banners for the Superbowl; and **Alterations by Caterina**, which is a unique tailoring service.

This book is sure to energize both immigrant and American-born communities, boost entrepreneurship, and enable future economic prosperity in our state. Through these stories and the empathy they cultivate, we are all able to reach across conceived borders to learn about one another, be inspired, and find the value in all of our contributions.

Dr. Rajiv Tandon
President, The Institute for Innovators and Entrepreneurs at Hamline University

Acknowledgments

To date, Green Card Voices (GCV) has recorded 350 stories of immigrants and refugees coming from 120 countries currently living in seven US states. Since our founding in 2013, we have focused on recording and sharing digital, first-person immigrant narratives, and since 2015 we have expanded our storytelling media to include traveling exhibits and first-person written anthologies. *Green Card Entrepreneur Voices: How-To Business Stories from Minnesota Immigrants* is our fifth title, following four *Green Card Youth Voices* books focused on different cities (Minneapolis, St. Paul, Fargo, and Atlanta).

In the past five years, some of the most amazing stories we have had the opportunity to record were those of immigrant entrepreneurs. Not only did their stories inform viewers about the immigrant journey, but they also provided a wealth of knowledge on how to build a business. With this book, we wanted to share the unique stories, knowledge that immigrant entrepreneurs hold, and give the storytellers a chance to tell their *own* stories.

First and foremost, this book would not be possible without the twenty immigrant entrepreneurs from across the state of Minnesota who shared their stories and their time. Their courage, ingenuity, and perseverance inspire us all; they are the heart and soul of this work. Through their efforts, we are able to transcend boundaries and learn about the truth of the human experience. We are honored to share their words in these pages.

In order to select the storytellers featured in this volume, we searched our own archive—stories we've recorded over the past five years—and sought out new stories recorded as recently as February 2018. For recordings made in past years, we consulted with the storytellers and assembled new material to bring their stories up to date. We also wanted to engage with people outside our network and create an opportunity for people to nominate an immigrant entrepreneur. Through this community effort and our own relationships, we were able to identify and select the twenty storytellers, originating from nineteen countries, that you see here. We also sought out diversity in terms of country of origin, gender, age, race, religion, industry, scope, scale, and size—including social entrepreneurs. We aim to share a vast breadth of experiences and demystify some of the prevalent stereotypes about immigrant entrepreneurs—ones that often overemphasize the "American Dream." In their own words, these immigrants' stories do just this.

During this time, our staff had many meetings with people who teach entrepreneurship throughout Minnesota and Wisconsin. We met with academic institutions, as well as various chambers and nonprofit organizations such as Metropolitan Economic Development Association (MEDA), that work directly with minority business owners. We would like to thank the chambers, MEDA, and the incredible people at the following schools: the University of Minnesota, St. Thomas University, Concordia College, Hamline University, and the University of Wisconsin–Eau Claire. All of these relationships were instrumental in moving this book forward.

We would like to thank Dr. Bruce Corrie, Jonathan Weinhagen, Johan Eriksson, M.P. Singh, and Dara Beevas for their input during initial advisory meetings.

We would like to thank our foreword author, Dr. Rajiv Tandon, an immigrant from India and a self-described advocate for the future of entrepreneurship in Minnesota. He is currently president of the Institute for Innovators and Entrepreneurs at Hamline University, cofounder of 100 Launches, founder of the Rocket Network, and author of a monthly opinion column called "Planting Seeds" in *Twin Cities Business Magazine* (This book will be featured in the June 2018 issue).

Many thanks also to Dr. Jay Ebben, associate professor of entrepreneurship at the University of St. Thomas, who wrote the introduction for *Green Card Entrepreneur Voices*. His intentional effort to learn about entrepreneurship in different cultures and countries drew us to him. He was critical in framing and providing context for these multicultural narratives.

We contracted with Media Active for most of the stories' video recordings. We especially want to thank Dominica Asberry-Lindquist, David Buchanan, Amal Flower-Kay, Tahiel Jimenez, Carmela Simione, Gabe Vargas, and Ahxuen Ybarra, who did the videography and photography, as well as Michael Hay for supervising. We would also like to thank Justin Evidon for additional media work.

Many thanks to our crew of transcribers, who spent hours listening to the audio from the interviews of the immigrant storytellers and helping us take their spoken words to the page. These individuals include: Anna Boyer, Kelly Rynda, Kathleen Kessler, Gloria Narabrook, Jonell L. Pacyga, Arazue Foroozan, Ilse H. Griffin, Molly Hill, Kara Hippen, Anna Hilbelink, Dana

Boyle, Meron Demissie, Raghu Aggarwal, Natanya Schnyer, and Zamzam Ahmed.

To the media contributors who saw the value in this work and spread the word through their publications, thank you! We would specifically like to thank Nick Williams at the *Minneapolis/St. Paul Business Journal.*

We began envisioning this book several years ago, but it would not have come to fruition without funding. We would like to thank Solidarity MN for an initial grant, all of our crowdfunding supporters (especially Brian Linne, Staphany Park, Ashley Wirth-Petrik, Dara Beevas, and Enrique Salazar), and all those who contributed to the book during the Fund-a-Need at Green Card Voices 2017 annual gala.

We would like to extend a sincere thank-you to the Green Card Voices team. José Guzmán, graphic designer and video editor, transformed raw video footage into compelling digital narratives and designed the interior of the book. Rachel Mueller, GCV program manager and coeditor for this book, did an extraordinary job of keeping the team on track and working one-on-one with the immigrant entrepreneurs to ensure their stories were accurately and inspiringly told. Special thanks goes to Raghu Aggarwal, who was incredibly helpful as assistant editor. We are thankful that Zamzam Ahmed joined the team as a program associate, and are excited to have her support for future programming. We extend deep gratitude to Dr. Tea Rozman-Clark, GCV cofounder, executive director, and coeditor, whose vision and leadership allowed for transformational, educational experiences for all involved. Her grace and commitment are inspiring.

Special thanks goes to Humphrey School of Public Policy students at the University of Minnesota, and Tea Rozman Clark's classroom peers: Joseph Schaefbauer and Claire Psarouthakis, for helping Green Card Voices envision a social entrepreneurial platform for immigrant entrepreneur voices. Similarly, we would like to thank Joelle Allen and her Integrated Marketing Communications class at the University of St. Thomas for helping us brainstorm potential markets for this book.

A tremendous thank-you goes to Dara Beevas, Patrick Maloney, and Graham Warnken at Wise Ink Creative Publishing for their advice, support, copyediting, and encouragement. Our collaboration, as well as their donations of time and consultation, greatly enhanced the final product.

Thank you to all of our Green Card Voices board members present— Jessica Cordova Kramer, Johan Eriksson, Masami Suga, George C. Maxwell,

Hibo Abdi, Ruben Hidalgo, Dana Boyle, Gregory Eagan IV, Debjyoti Dwivedy, and Mahlet Aschenaki—and past—Miguel Ramos, Veronica Quillien, Katie Murphy-Olsen, Jane Graupman, Ali Alizadeh, Laura Danielson, Jeff Corn, Ruhel Islam, Angela Eifert, Matt Kim, Tara Kennedy, and Kathy Seipp—and all the others who have helped our mission along the way.

Introduction

For several centuries, the United States has had immigrants arriving at its shores. However, common narratives gloss over the significant impact of the individual lives of America's new arrivals even though our multicultural and ethnically diverse population has always been one of the country's greatest assets. Often forgotten in these narratives, but equally important to remember, are the Native Americans who are the original people of this land and the descendants of the Africans who were brought here against their will.

According to the US Census Bureau, an estimated 13.4 percent of our population today, or 43.2 million people, were not born in the United States, and immigration to the United States is increasing—by 2050, one in five Americans will be an immigrant.[1] This trend is consistent with other moments of growth that have strengthened the United States in the past.

As a country of immigrants, it should be no surprise that many of our economic, technological, and social advancements are due to the efforts of immigrant entrepreneurs. In fact, there are many contemporary examples of prominent companies such as Uber, WhatsApp, Google, and PayPal—some of whose products we use every day—that were founded by immigrants. There are many not-as-contemporary household brands as well, including Intel, Kohl's, and AT&T.

The statistics regarding immigrant entrepreneurs speak to this. Over the past twenty years, the rate of new entrepreneurs among US-born citizens has held steady at just under 0.3 percent of the population, but the percentage of immigrants who start businesses has grown from 0.36 percent in 1996 to around 0.52 percent in 2014.[2] It is estimated that immigrants now start approximately one out of every four new businesses in the US despite making up only 13 percent of the overall population.[3]

Why are immigrants more likely to start a business than American-born individuals? According to Dr. Rajiv Tandon, discrimination in labor markets may exert pressure on many immigrants to seek self-employment.

1. López, G. and Radford, J. (2017, May). Facts on U.S. Immigrants, 2015: Statistical Portrait of the Foreign Born Population in the United States. Pew Research Center: Hispanic Trends. Retrieved from www.pewhispanic.org/2017/05/03/facts-on-u-s-immigrants-current-data/
2. Wiens, J., Jackson, C., and Fetsch, E. (2015, January). Immigrant Entrepreneurs: A Path to U.S. Economic Growth. Kauffman Foundation. Retrieved from www.kauffman.org/what-we-do/resources/entrepreneurship-policy-digest/immigrant-entrepreneurs-a-path-to-us-economic-growth
3. Miller, D. (2017, July). Why Immigrant Entrepreneurs are Crucial for America's Future. National Venture Capital Association. Retrieved from nvca.org/blog/immigrant-entrepreneurs-crucial-americas-future/

For others, cross-cultural experiences increase their capabilities to find new niches, serve existing customers differently, connect with different markets, access distinct networks, or invent different business models. Leaving your home for another country is inherently risky; as such, the uncertainty associated with starting a business does not seem as formidable.

These immigrant-founded firms include a significant number of large and high-growth companies. 40 percent of Fortune 500 companies have a first- or second-generation immigrant among their founders,[1] and over 20 percent of the 500 fastest-growing firms in 2014 had immigrant CEOs.[2] Immigrant entrepreneurs founded 31 percent of all venture-capital-funded firms, as well as 51 percent of the US start-ups valued at $1 billion or more.[3]

Small firms started by immigrants are just as important. There are 900,000 immigrant small-business owners in the US (small firms are those with fewer than 100 employees), and immigrant small-business owners accounted for 30 percent of the growth in the number of small businesses in the U.S. between 1990 and 2010; these immigrant-owned small firms employed 4.7 million people in 2007.[4] Immigrants are also starting businesses at a disproportionate rate in some of the fastest-growing sectors in the US, such as health care, professional services, and education services.[5] Immigrant-owned small businesses make up a disproportionate percentage of other sectors as well, with immigrants making up 61 percent of all gas station owners, 58 percent of dry-cleaning owners, 53 percent of grocery store owners, and 38 percent of restaurant owners.[6]

The positive impact of these firms on our economy is impressive. In general, younger firms exhibit much higher job growth than more mature firms, with new and small firms accounting for over two-thirds of the net job growth in the US.[7] Specific to immigrant-founded firms, one in ten Americans who work for a private company is employed by an immigrant-owned busi-

1. Leadem, R. (2017, February). The Immigrant Entrepreneurs Behind Major American Companies. Entrepreneur. Retrieved from www.entrepreneur.com/article/288687

2. Bluestein, A. (2015, January). The Most Entrepreneurial Group in America Wasn't Born in America. Inc.com. Retrieved from www.inc.com/magazine/201502/adam-bluestein/the-most-entrepreneurial-group-in-america-wasnt-born-in-america.html

3. Koh, Y. (2017, March). Study: Immigrants Founded 51% of U.S. Billion-Dollar Startups. Wall Street Journal. Retrieved from blogs.wsj.com/digits/2016/03/17/study-immigrants-founded-51-of-u-s-billion-dollar-startups/

4. Fiscal Policy Institute (2012, June). Immigrant Small Business Owners: A Significant and Growing Part of the Economy. Retrieved from www.fiscalpolicy.org/immigrant-small-business-owners-FPI-20120614.pdf

5. New American Economy (2012, August). How Immigrants are Driving Small Business Creation in the United States. Retrieved from www.newamericaneconomy.org/sites/all/themes/pnae/openforbusiness.pdf

6. Gibble, E. (2016, May). Celebrate National Small Business Week With These Facts About Immigrant Economic Contributions. American Immigration Council. Retrieved from immigrationimpact.com/2016/05/03/immigrant-small-business-owners/

7. Decker, R., Haltiwanger, J., Jarmin, R., and Miranda, J. (2014). The Role of Entrepreneurship in U.S. Job Creation and Economic Dynamism. Journal of Economic Perspectives. 28(3), 3-24.

ness, and these businesses pay an estimated $126 billion in wages per year.[8] The fastest-growing venture-capital-backed firms founded by immigrants have created an average of 150 jobs per company, and in the engineering and high-tech sectors alone, these firms employed 50,000 workers and generated $63 billion in sales in 2012.[9]

This positive economic impact extends beyond job creation and wages. Immigrant founders play a significant role in connecting the US to global markets—this is important, as about half of US economic growth has come from exports in the past few years. Immigrant-led businesses are 60 percent more likely to export than those led by native-born Americans, and they are over 2.5 times more likely to have exports make up a large portion of their sales.[10]

Here in Minnesota, the impact of immigrant entrepreneurs is similar, with the Minnesota Chamber of Commerce report concluding that "Minnesota's immigrant communities are critical to the state's economic success". Six of Minnesota's Fortune 500 companies were founded by first- or second-generation immigrants, and these firms employ over 200,000 people globally.[11] Overall, there are over 16,000 immigrant entrepreneurs in the state, whose firms employ over 50,000 Minnesotans.[12] These entrepreneurs have transformed commercial corridors such as University Avenue in Saint Paul and Lake Street in Minneapolis, and are an established presence in smaller cities including Willmar, Austin, Worthington, and Faribault-Northfield.

There is good reason to embrace this impact. While Minnesota's economy is relatively strong, the last Fortune 500 Company to be born in Minnesota was in the 1970s, and the rate of new startups in Minnesota has declined relative to the rest of the US. Without the growth of immigrant-owned businesses, Minnesota's economic outlook could be much worse. Nationwide, we have witnessed a decline in our global share of venture capital from 80 percent of funding activity here in the US to just 54 percent, with China and Europe

8. Bluestein, A. (2015, January). The Most Entrepreneurial Group in America Wasn't Born in America. Inc.com. Retrieved from www.inc.com/magazine/201502/adam-bluestein/the-most-entrepreneurial-group-in-america-wasnt-born-in-america.html

9. Wiens, J., Jackson, C., and Fetsch, E. (2015, January). Immigrant Entrepreneurs: A Path to U.S. Economic Growth. Kauffman Foundation. Retrieved from www.kauffman.org/what-we-do/resources/entrepreneurship-policy-digest/immigrant-entrepreneurs-a-path-to-us-economic-growth

10. Bluestein, A. (2015, January). The Most Entrepreneurial Group in America Wasn't Born in America. Inc.com. Retrieved from www.inc.com/magazine/201502/adam-bluestein/the-most-entrepreneurial-group-in-america-wasnt-born-in-america.html

11. New American Economy (2016, August). The Contributions of New Americans in Minnesota. Retrieved from www.newamericaneconomy.org/wp-content/uploads/2017/02/nae-mn-report.pdf

12. Williams, N. (2017, February). As Trump Administration cracks down, Minnesota Chamber touts value of immigrants. Minneapolis/St. Paul Business Journal. Retrieved from www.bizjournals.com/twincities/news/2017/02/21/as-trump-administration-cracks-down-minnesota.html

taking much of that share.[13] For these reasons, policies around attracting and retaining immigrant entrepreneurs, such as the H-1 visa, are currently garnering significant attention.

But the importance of this book is not about statistics or even the impact made by immigrants. It is about capturing what lies beneath, about capturing the human stories that make up the statistics. We have many stereotypes about entrepreneurs in general, and many more about immigrants. Through storytelling, we are able to demystify who immigrant entrepreneurs are, connect with them, and operate with a more open mindset and gain a better understanding of how immigrants contribute.

Green Card Voices (GCV) has worked tirelessly to humanize the debates surrounding immigrants, refugees, and their families in order to better integrate all of our communities. GCV actively works to combat stereotypes and create empathy through an online video platform, published books, seven sets of traveling exhibits, in-person storytelling events, and a soon-to-be-released podcast. *Green Card Entrepreneur Voices: How-To Business Stories from Minnesota Immigrants* focuses on bringing the stories of the most entrepreneurial population of America to the forefront, in the words of the immigrant entrepreneurs themselves. The GCV process, which typically involves asking all the storytellers six open-ended questions, was expanded upon for this book to capture the unique insight of immigrant entrepreneurs. By adding an additional three questions where the storytellers were asked to reflect specifically on their entrepreneur journeys, and then turning the transcripts from these interviews into the personal essays you read here, GCV aims to put the storytellers' step-by-step instructions into a worldly context. This is a book about immigrants, written by immigrants, but it is also a book about entrepreneurs—what they have done, how they have done it, and what they have learned.

Here you will read stories of people who spent years in refugee camps before finally arriving in the US with just a suitcase, who earned university degrees in different countries only to move here to find they didn't carry weight. There are stories about the quest to find the perfect career and making multiple false starts along the way. There are stories about discrimination and hardships in school and in the workplace. There are stories about failing and about success. And, of course, there are stories about how cold that first winter in Minnesota was. In these pages, you will find social entrepreneurs and small-business owners who have developed products that support their home country

13. Miller, D. (2017, July). Why Immigrant Entrepreneurs are Crucial for America's Future. National Venture Capital Association. Retrieved from nvca.org/blog/immigrant-entrepreneurs-crucial-americas-future/

communities and have built new organizations in the US based on their own cultural traditions.

The circumstances around which they came to the United States, the experiences they had when they arrived, and the reasons for and ambitions in starting a business vary from person to person. And you will see that the people in these stories are not so different from you or me: they are shaped by their past, they lead with their values, and their successes are a result of their own initiative.

It is in the humanization of statistics that we realize that every story, and every person behind each story, contributes uniquely to the tapestry of our nation. So, read these stories with an open mind, allow yourself to connect with the individuals, be inspired by what they have been able to achieve, and embrace the positive impact they make. And recognize the fact that we all have a unique story, we all have the ability to inspire, and we all can achieve whatever it is we set out to do.

Tea Rozman Clark
Rachel Mueller
Green Card Voices

Dr. Jay Ebben
University of St. Thomas

How to Use this Book

At the end of each storyteller's essay, you will find a URL link to that entrepreneur's digital narrative and podcast on Green Card Voices' website. You will also see a QR code link to that story. Below are instructions for using your mobile device to scan a QR code.

1.Using your mobile device—such as a smartphone or tablet—visit the App Store for your operating system, such as the Apple Store or the Android Store. Search the App Store for a "QR reader." You will find multiple free apps to download, and any one of them will work with this book.

2. Open your new QR reader app. Once the app has opened, hover the camera on your mobile device a few inches away from the QR code you want to scan. The app will capture the image of the QR code and take you to that entrepreneur's profile page on the Green Card Voices website.

3. Once your web browser opens, you'll see the digital story and podcast. Press play and watch or listen to one of our inspirational stories.

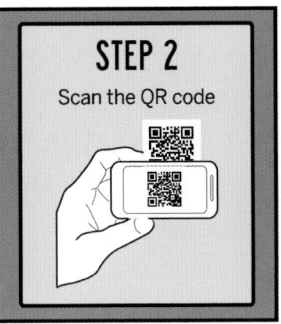
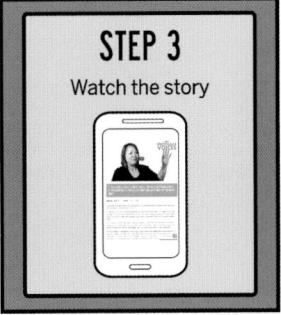

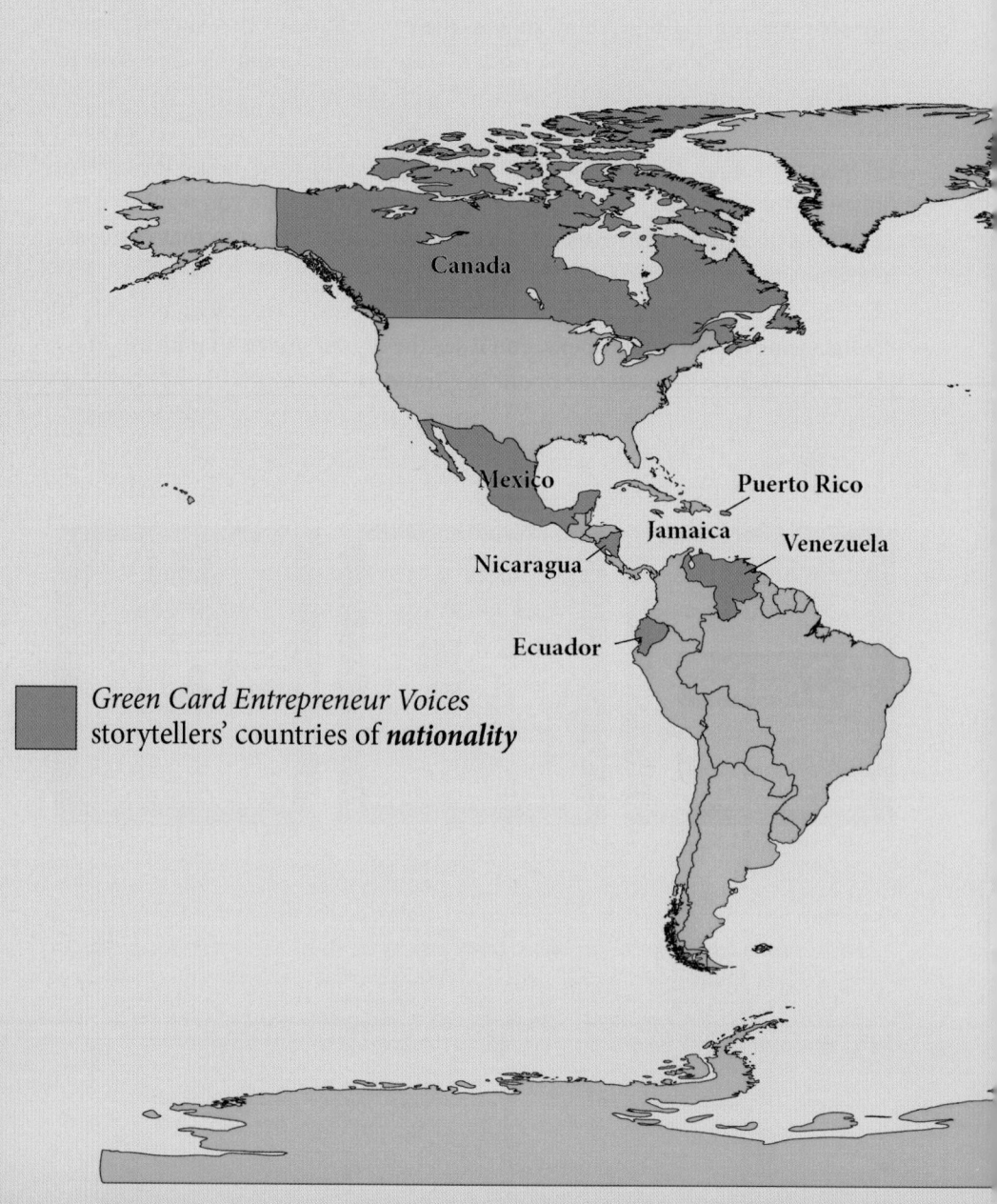

Canada

Mexico

Puerto Rico

Jamaica

Venezuela

Nicaragua

Ecuador

Green Card Entrepreneur Voices
storytellers' countries of ***nationality***

World Map

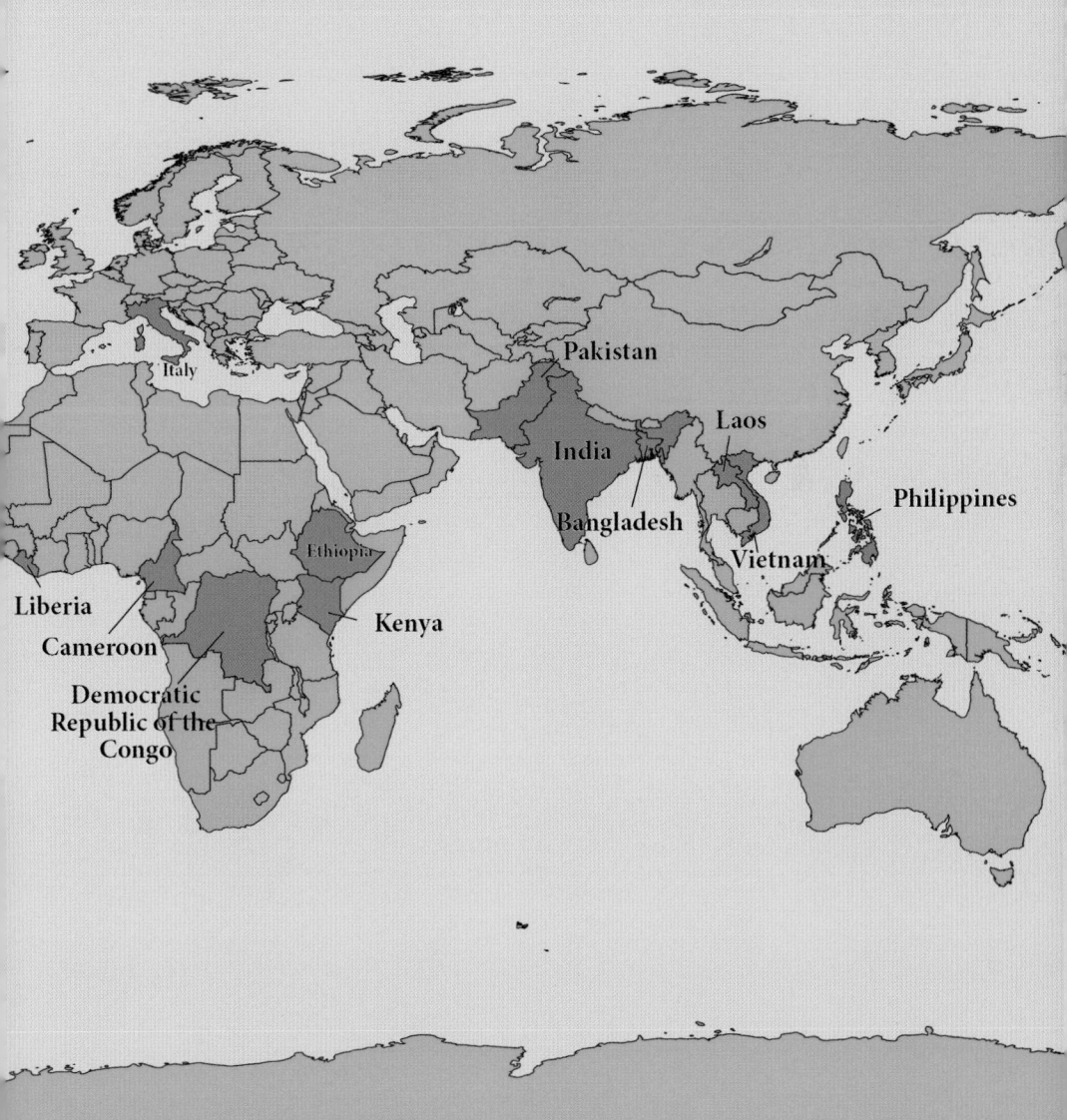

Personal Essays

Aloo,
Ethiopia

Tashitaa Tufaa

From: Aloo, Ethiopia
Current City: Champlin, MN

Current Business:
Metropolitan Transportation Network
metrotn.com

> "I WASN'T ALWAYS AN ENTREPRENEUR, BUT I WAS A FAST MOVER, AN ACTION-TAKER. MY FRIENDS AND PARENTS ALWAYS TOLD ME I WAS TOO FAST."

I was born and raised in a village in Ethiopia. My parents had fourteen children. We lived on a farm, so as a young boy, I worked on the farm, then went to school, and then came back and worked on the farm some more. I also played soccer. When I was in junior elementary school, we had to move to another village, and for high school, I had to go to the city. I went back home during the weekends and worked on the farm some more; that is how it was.

Growing up on a farm is challenging. You start working at a very early age and only have two hours a day to go to the field and play soccer. I learned the value of hard work; you have no choice but to finish what you're given. For example, my responsibilities started when I was six. I had to look after goats and sheep. They were easy to take care of. One day a fox came and ate a baby sheep while I was sitting there. The fox undermined me, and knew I couldn't do anything to her. I hid this from my parents when I headed home. I was punished when the baby sheep was gone; they thought I couldn't take care of it.

Ethiopia was a communist country at the time. Not many opportunities were available. My extended family sponsored my education at an American college in Zimbabwe. I went to that school and finished my bachelor's degree there. Then I went back to Ethiopia and worked at the Seventh Day Adventist High School as a history and English teacher for a year. I went to another school, the Yemen Arab Community School, and taught there for another year prior to coming to the United States.

There was great unrest in Ethiopia when I decided to move to the United States. I was a very politically oriented, educated young man. I strongly disagreed with the regime. I never agreed with the Ethiopian government, past or present. The country was operated by an oppressive, dictatorial government, and still is. I knew from the very beginning that I did not have any place there. I got a United States visa, and I knew when I left that I was not going to come back. I came to Minnesota and settled here.

I knew the United States was a place where there were so many opportunities. There were people from other countries and from my own country. I didn't think there was any better place. I came to Minnesota because my older sister was here, as well as my cousins and other extended family.

I left Addis Ababa on August 16, 1992. I spent a night in Frankfurt, one of the most beautiful cities in the world. It was the first time I saw a developed Western city. Going from the airport to the hotel and then from the hotel to the airport, I loved it. I still would like to go back and see it again. I went from Frankfurt to Chicago; then I had to travel from Chicago to Minneapolis the same day.

Back home in Ethiopia, there is group life and many people have a lot of time to waste. When I came back there from Zimbabwe, I had to live in the city, where you could just walk around after you came back from work. But when I moved to the United States, there was no time to do that. You can't really waste your time here. You have to focus and plan your future, and that is exactly what I did.

I arrived in Minneapolis in August 1992 at 1401 Portland Avenue South, Apartment C 201. I lived in a low-income apartment building downtown. My place was the most beautiful apartment I had ever seen. I had never seen an apartment like that prior, so I knew that America was different.

Of course, English was very challenging. I knew I had to learn written English, and I thought I could speak English and maybe even teach it back home. But then I came here and felt like I didn't know English. I had to focus on my language skills as well as how I could go forward and join a graduate school.

I got a work permit. The same day, I went out and applied for a job. The Minneapolis Hilton had just been built, and they were hiring dishwashers and cleaners. I got hired for the second shift as a dishwasher for $5.65 an hour, which was the greatest job ever for me.

There are many opportunities in this country, but at the same time good jobs are not available to immigrants. In the US, you have to do labor, be a housekeeper or a dishwasher or security guard; those are the jobs available to you, other opportunities are not. I wanted to be a diplomat, but I was not a US citizen. I had to look at things differently. I had to be creative, and as a result there were other opportunities around me.

I planned to go to graduate school, which was very challenging because of my poor English skills, but eventually I was admitted as a part-time student. I had to take a course to prove I was able to complete graduate work. Then I did a second, and then a third. I got good grades, and then I was admitted.

When I went to graduate school, I was also working as a security guard and a housekeeper. When I was acting as security, I was also taking advantage of the time, doing my homework as I sat at the desk. I also worked for the university, escorting girls at night when they came out of the library and taking them back to their dormitories.

After finishing school, I had a chance; I was hired by the Minneapolis School District to help principals and teachers with children who had behavioral problems. I had wonderful interpersonal skills, and by this time my English had also improved. I would take the children who had bad behavior and trouble focusing in school to my office, and could very easily calm them down and take them back to school. I guess that was a gift that I had.

As I was doing that, I was also in a civil service job that would only pay me for 38.75 hours weekly, not forty hours. Eventually, the principal at Anderson Open School told me, "Stay longer. I know you are a professional, and I know you have a young child. You need more hours, so I will give you forty hours." Forty hours was more than anybody else in the district got at that time. He decided to give me forty-three hours of work even though everybody else could only work less than forty hours. This was a great opportunity.

I used to work eight hours a day and go home; it was not enough, so to supplement my income I decided to find a second job, which was driving the Metro Mobility bus after work. During the weekend, I could still do over forty hours with overtime, and I started making more money. What helped me do more hours was the fact that I grew up in a village doing very hard farm work; it made everything that I did very simple for me.

I worked for about seven years in the school district; finally, I left and went to the Minneapolis Housing Authority. I worked there for two years. I was still driving, but then I lost my professional civil service job in about 2002. I asked myself then, "What are my skills? What's a job where I could still drive the bus and put bread on the table for my family? Well, if I can drive a bus well, can't I also find my own business and do it? Why not?" Then I started Metropolitan Transportation Network with my wife's minivan and the taxicab I owned.

That's where I am now. My children, and my other two children who I adopted from my older brother, go to a boarding school in Hutchinson, Minnesota. It's about a ninety minute drive from my home. I take my children there and visit them most weekends. There are so many school activities that I have to be involved in. We all go to church, and then after church we go to a farm together; I grew up a farm boy and I still love farms. In the summertime, my hobbies are driving out to the farm and looking at the animals, the cornfields, and everything else.

I wasn't always an entrepreneur, but I was a fast mover, an action-taker. My friends and parents always told me I was too fast. A lot of people don't agree with me, because I take actions faster than others around me. What I have learned from my entrepreneurial journey is that you have to be patient, but you also you have to take action quickly. You have to work hard and respond to customers in a quick, professional way. You have to sometimes compromise your other values and concentrate on growing your business. For example, when it comes to family, two of my children were born as I was working. My wife was giving birth at the hospital and I was not able to be with her, but she could still understand.

Don't complain. Take advantage of the opportunities you have. Opportunities may be around the corner and you may not understand them yet. Do not look for a bigger opportunity when smaller chances around you could make you a fortune. When it comes to business, sometimes you have to spit food out of your mouth to answer a phone call from your customer. What I mean is, don't be very comfortable. You have to be uncomfortable to jump into opportunities.

For example, if you have a good job that pays you well with benefits, it is hard to leave and find a better opportunity. So don't be comfortable where you are. When opportunities come and you are starting a business, make sure you pay other people before you pay yourself. The profit you make in the beginning shouldn't be spent on luxuries but should be invested back into your business. Make sure you do your books honestly. If you're trying to hide from the government and not pay taxes, you will be punished one way or another. Do not mess with the IRS. Hire and consult with a good accountant who will give you good advice, and listen instead of telling them what to do.

I believe I was born to give. I give to my community in many different ways. As a businessman, I make a lot of contributions to young sports clubs, like the soccer club. I give money to communities, mosques, and churches. I give back to the schools. I was a board member of a few schools in the metro area. I also do volunteer service in the community. I make time to go out and work in my community.

MEDIA LINKS

greencardvoices.org/speakers/tashitaa-tufaa

Luang Prabang,
Laos

Bo Thao-Urabe

From: Luang Prabang, Laos

Current City: Eagan, MN

Current Business:

RedGreen Rivers

redgreenrivers.com

> "I'VE LEARNED ALONG THE WAY THAT YOU CAN'T BE THE ONE TO GIVE UP ON YOUR IDEAS. THERE ARE PLENTY OF PEOPLE WHO WILL DOUBT YOU AND EVEN BLOW YOU OFF, BUT YOU HAVE TO BELIEVE IN WHAT YOU'RE TRYING TO DO."

The relationship between the United States and Laos changed my destiny forever. My experiences and my personal journey to discover my gifts have driven me to create and produce social good through both for-profit and nonprofit businesses.

I was born in Laos in Luang Prabang Province in the midst of the Secret War, a covert operation led by the US Central Intelligence Agency. The CIA recruited our Hmong people into special guerrilla units in order to stop military supply movements from North to South Vietnam and to rescue downed American pilots. It was a "secret war" because no foreign troops were supposed to be in Laos during the Vietnam War. As it turned out, diplomatic agreements aren't always honored, and both the US and Vietnam were very present in Laos.

In 1975, the Vietnam War ended and the US left. In Laos, the US rescued a few planes full of high-ranking Hmong officers and their families but left the rest of the foot soldiers and their families, like mine, to fend for themselves. With no more American support or presence, the Communists took over Laos. Soon they announced that they would punish those who sided with the Americans. Re-education camps opened and people were arrested and sent there. Others decided to make their way to Thailand; still others continued fighting to see if they could stay on the land they had called home for generations.

My father left my mother alone with us—four small children aged four, three, two, and less than a year—as he went on fighting. After several months, my mother sensed that it was no longer safe to stay in our village, so she took us into the jungle to hide and wait for my father's return. There we hid for several months. No longer able to farm, my mother would hide us under banana leaves each night after we fell asleep, then go off to find food.

After several months in the jungle, a group of Hmong families came across us and asked my mother why we had not yet left Laos. She explained that we were waiting for my father. An elderly man told my mother he had received news that Communist soldiers were nearing our location—we had to leave or we would all be killed. This man had the same clan name as my mother, so he told her to consider him a relative and leave with his group—he would help carry my little sister. My mother took him up on his offer, and that's how we left Laos. We had no idea if we would see my father again.

We walked in complete darkness every night for a month, crossing farmland and wandering up and down mountains and rivers. We finally arrived at the Thai border, and my father miraculously found us before we were sent to Ban Nam Yao Refugee Camp in northern Thailand.

In one small room, our family of six (which eventually became seven) lived for three years in Ban Nam Yao. My only memories from that time are of the hot weather, the dirt and muddiness during monsoon season, the crowds, and being hungry almost all the time. I was always the child who waited in the food ration line with my mother. After my parents began the application process to be resettled in America, we were poked and examined for three years before finally being approved to go. It felt as if we might never leave that place.

With no means to make money, my mother started to sew handicrafts known as *paj ntauj* (flower cloth) to sell to Christians who came to the camp. Soon my father was sewing too. I remember thinking this was unusual because traditionally only women sewed the flower cloths, but when you have no other way to earn, you use every asset you have. Women and their husbands sitting together, sewing what their minds could imagine for their new customers, became a normal scene within the camp. I would later learn that Christians went to the refugee camps where there were Hmong people to buy up as many *paj ntaub* as possible. This enterprise became a primary means of helping families earn income to buy medicine, food, and other necessities. Eventually some were even able to earn enough to start their own small businesses inside the refugee camps.

Our family was finally approved to come to America in December 1979. We packed up our belongings into one plastic bag and boarded a large bus to take us to Bangkok in order to fly to America. That was my first time on a plane. I was so nauseous the whole trip that I couldn't eat anything the whole flight over.

As winter began, we arrived in Chicago to mountains of snow. The only other time I had seen snow was when vendors came into the refugee camp to sell snow cones. It almost seemed magical that I had access to so much of it now, but we were told not to eat it.

Chicago was so far from the world I knew. I had never seen skyscrapers, elevators, or so many cars. I thought if you got into an elevator, you would change and become someone else. There were so many things that were new and foreign to me, but we adjusted the best we could. Soon there was a little community of other Hmong refugees who made their way to Chicago.

My father started work, my mother began an English class, and we, the kids, began school. On our first day of school, our family sponsor dropped us off and the principal walked us to class. I was taken to a desk and sat down. I could see that all the students were staring at me. I looked at what they were doing and saw that a sheet of dotted letters was on my desk. I began to trace the alphabet.

My mother found a job cleaning houses. She was told to take the public bus to work, but she had no idea how. On her first day of work, she took me along—I guess she figured my English was better than hers, so I could help her navigate. Together we got on the bus and rode. She didn't know where to stop and I didn't know how to ask for help, so we quietly rode on and on. Eventually, the bus came to a stop and the bus driver told us to get off. We didn't know why, but now I can only assume that he was done with his route. He looked at my mother's address and showed my mother how to get on another bus to the house. Just recalling my mother's sheer determination makes me realize the conviction she had to do her best so she could take care of her family.

We lived in Chicago for a few years, then moved to Little Chute, Wisconsin, a tiny, rural town with one stoplight. That was another culture shock, because we no longer saw black people. On our first day in our little house, the neighbor brought a pie. I think she was just as shocked to see that we were not a white family as we were by her bringing us food.

In middle school, I started to have recurring nightmares. In one dream, my mother and brother fell into a river and started drowning. In the second dream, a baby was hysterically crying and there was nothing I could do. After several months of having these nightmares and always waking up crying, I finally asked my mother about them. She told me that they were not nightmares but real events that had happened during our month long walk to Thailand.

It turns out that she and my brother fell into a river as we were walking on the side of a hill. Because she couldn't swim, they almost drowned before being rescued. As for the baby, he was a child left behind on the road because he was constantly crying. The whole group was in danger because the child could not be quiet, so the mother was given a choice—leave the child or stay behind with the child. In agony, the mother chose to leave the baby behind. My three-year-old mind must have somehow buried the memories in my subconscious, only for them to resurface in my teens. Learning the truth didn't make things better, but at least I had a better understanding of where these dreams were coming from.

In Wisconsin, my mother figured out that we could start farming again. She found a cucumber farmer who rented us several acres of land for the summer. We weren't old enough to work, but we were old enough to be extra sets of hands at the farm. We spent whole summers farming cucumber, then ginseng, then corn. We knew the money we made was not for us, but for the family, so never saw any of it.

We moved to St. Paul, Minnesota when I started high school because my father wanted to go to a trade school to learn auto-body detailing work. This meant leaving behind our extended family in Wisconsin, but my father needed to earn more to support us, and he liked cars. With no real options in Wisconsin for someone with no formal education, he was convinced that St. Paul was it. There was yet again a new environment we had to adjust to. For the first time I was in school with many students who looked like me and shared my family's story.

By second grade, I spoke more English than my parents, so I became their interpreter everywhere—at the hospital, at school, at McDonald's. Aunts and uncles would be waiting for me after school to help them read their mail or complete paperwork. I was an angry teen then and would be so upset, because all I knew was that my other teenage friends were not doing what I was doing. My mother let me vent and then said something that has stuck with me until this day. She told me, "You should be grateful that you have a skill that people need, and they find you useful. When you're no longer useful, you don't mean really anything to the community." I stopped complaining after that.

Through a lot of trial and error, I have become a version of what I consider a global citizen. As I reflect on my journey now, I see a girl trying to discover herself. Along the way she shares her challenges, gives a voice to the realities of her struggles, and then works to find solutions. Sometimes alone but often with others, she's persistent and has the conviction to keep going. I've repeated this cycle of problem-solving over and over.

I also see the privileges I have in America and the opportunities that would never have been afforded me had our family not come. When I went back to Laos for the first time in 2003, I saw many Hmong women my age who were struggling so much. When I saw them, I saw myself; they had just been on the other side of the war. So I asked, "What can I do? How do I bring our worlds closer together?"

Asking these questions has led me to create many types of answers. What I've been most proud of is that those answers have produced both financial and social returns. I've helped structure for- and nonprofit businesses. I love what I do because it gives back to the community. I also feel extremely lucky that I've worked with so many people and organizations who want to ensure that all people in this country are able to fully contribute and build the future.

Another pivotal growth moment for me was moving away from my family on my own. I moved to Green Bay after college, then to DC and New York. I really felt like I wouldn't grow unless I moved away. All I had known my whole life up to that point was that having the support of a family was everything, but I needed to be strong on my own. My parents were worried as any parent would be, but I think when you've had the kind of traumatic experiences my parents had, you worry even more. Add that to a culture that doesn't accept that women should be single or on their own and one can understand why wanting to be an independent and strong woman seems almost impossible.

A challenge faced by immigrant entrepreneurs that I've observed is that we may not always get the systemic help we need. We're good about taking all the risk ourselves and usually make no demands from the system to make it work better for us. For example, we often self-finance because we may not know what options there are for loans or investments that exist to help us get started or grow.

Five years ago, I started a giving circle that brings together people who want to pool their money together to support existing projects and non-

Cuenca,
Ecuador

that I meet or the children that come to our dance studio. The children might have a different perspective from their parents. I don't know what their home life is like, but I can only hope and pray that we create a positive safe place at the dance studio.

There's a wide range of people that have inspired me, everyone from Nelson Mandela to Tina Turner and Cher to Ché Guevara, Margot Fonteyn, and Maya Angelou. They all had a good sense of who they were; they had integrity. The way many countries, including the United States, view immigrants has changed, and I am noticing more and more that it's a difficult topic to have conversation about. I don't mind opening the conversation, most of all when it's a personal story I get to tell, a personal success story.

I would like to contribute to society by pursuing my love of dance, the medium through which I choose to communicate with people on a professional level. I also want to choreograph, compose, and direct things that have vibrant Ecuadorian traditions mixed with all other forms of traditional dance that I've seen here in the United States.

Since I have been given an education in dance, I'm able to take capoeira, a movement from traditional street fighting in Brazil, and mix it with break dancing. Fused together, the effect is striving for the impossible, creating a vibrant dance form. Another example of fusion would be mixing Chinese martial arts with hip-hop dancing, so you take some of the similar movements and put it to music—I think we even used Justin Timberlake the last time. There was a kind of serene, beautiful, organic, gentle feeling mixed with strong, striking, Chinese martial arts. It has opened my eyes up to the many different vibrant cultures in the world, and I have tried to learn and accept them with an open mind.

What I have learned the most is that, although life might not be fair, there's a silver lining in the end. You can continue to strive for greatness, although it might not be always recognized or cared about. For instance, I can put on huge performances and produce shows with my sister, and I recognize their artistic value. I can understand their relevance and why they are important to the community. There may be people who brush them off and think, "Oh, twinkle toes." But if I do an entire show and even one child is inspired to do something a little more extraordinary tomorrow, I see that as a success. I am not here to change the entire world, but my small influence can branch out and make a difference over the course of time. It certainly takes a long time, but I just wake up every day trying and trying again.

In the field of dance, there's a lot of division—for instance, the value of doing tricks compared to the artistry of being able to display expressions and emotions. I haven't been one to focus on one or the other just to get a quick thrill out of people, although I like to incorporate them into performances. I guess the right time and right place to do a trick is essential because you're also trying to get a message across, not just thrill the audience and have them forget about it. I like to have a lasting impact, which is why many of the dances I do are politically charged or have a really important message. Some people will open their eyes, but not everyone will experience it in the same way. I guess that's the ongoing reason you've got to persevere. We forget, degenerate, and eventually return to what we were before, like a phoenix.

Here I am. I don't necessarily feel special, but I do feel lucky every day to be in the situation I am. I have a home in Stillwater, I am grateful for my wit and character. I have a business, and we all work tirelessly to keep it running as entrepreneurs. My life here in the United States is pretty simple. I have all the basic necessities met; I have all of my wants taken care of, for the most part; and I'm able to just dream. I'm able to dream of what else I can take on.

greencardvoices.org/speakers/dario-mejia

Hyderabad,
Pakistan

Hassan Syed

From: Hyderabad, Pakistan
Current City: Minneapolis, MN

Current Business:
IdeaGist
ideagist.com

> "ENTREPRENEURSHIP IS A CONSTANT DANCE BETWEEN SUCCESS AND FAILURE. YOU CAN'T MAINTAIN THAT UNLESS YOU HAVE SOMETHING THAT IS DRIVING YOU; OTHERWISE YOU WILL VERY QUICKLY GET BOGGED DOWN BY THE FAILURES AND THE ROADBLOCKS YOU ARE FACING."

My name is Hassan Syed. I was born in Hyderabad, Pakistan, which used to be the third-largest city in the country. I grew up in a middle-class family. My dad and mom were both teachers, so we had books all over our house—in every cabinet and under every chair and sofa. That is how I grew up.

When I was about to get to high school, my dad won our city's first mayoral election. He became a member of the National Assembly afterward, and then Federal Minister. That was a very good experience, but it was also very heartbreaking, because there are lots of people who have challenges, and the government cannot solve all of them. The corruption in the system was an opportunity to learn, but at the same time you also felt really, really bad about it. That experience helped me to understand why it matters to help other people. That has been the driving force for me ever since. School was a really good opportunity for me to learn about what people were experiencing. You don't get exposed to a lot of that unless you see people coming and talking about their stories like they did at school.

After completing high school, I got a diploma in computer science; this was in the very early days of computer science. In Pakistan, there weren't a lot of big opportunities. I got a good start over there as a computer software developer, but to explore better opportunities, my sister, who was living in Bahrain, told me that I might want to come over there.

So I went to Bahrain on a visitor visa and was lucky to get a job right away. I worked there for a couple of years and then I worked for a multinational company. It was a Danish company, which gave me the opportunity to go to Denmark. In 1993, I felt I knew the system in Bahrain, and it was not a democratic system. Every day, I felt that something was not right. I am a person who loves his freedom, so I decided to move somewhere else. I decided Canada was the destination where I could start my family.

I applied for a Canadian visa and got it in three months. They didn't even ask any questions. I came to Canada in 1994, and that is where I started my family. All three of my kids were born in Canada. First I got a job at Kellogg's, and then in 1995 I started a company called Zentech Corporation, which was basically an ERP software company. I ran that company until 2002. In 2002, after the bubble burst and all the problems came for the technology companies, I went through a rough time. I thought, "Enough of doing this business. Maybe I should do something more meaningful."

I joined the Toronto Zoo as their manager for IT and communications, which was an amazing experience. I really enjoyed learning there, and in 2003, I came to the US for a conference on zoos and aquariums. There was a small organization from here in Minnesota at the conference, talking about building this big system for all the zoos to be able to share their data worldwide. I thought it was amazing and started participating in the project. Eventually they had an opening for somebody to lead that project—I applied for it and got it. I came to Minneapolis—the only city where I have lived in the US, where my kids have grown up, the city that love—to help zoos all over the world get their act together from a technology perspective and better share knowledge among themselves.

I've felt a huge culture shock over the years. Every place is different, but human beings are the same. When I went from Pakistan to Bahrain, the biggest challenge was language. English is not a language that you speak every day in Pakistan. I grew up speaking my language, Urdu, and then another language, Sindhi. Because my dad was an Arabic language teacher, he taught me Arabic when I was a kid. I came to Bahrain with the idea that they spoke Arabic. Instead, I got there and realized that the language I'd learned is really not the language that is spoken. Things were done totally different in Bahrain.

The biggest challenge for me at that time was to learn English. I remember my first job: the general manager of the company, a software company, said, "Hassan, I want you to go in front of the customers, but your English is not good." He gave me three months to get better at English. So I would wake up at five o'clock in the morning and would start watching the BBC. During lunch in Bahrain, it was common to have a siesta in the afternoon; people would go back to their home and come back later. I would watch the BBC then, and would come back in the evening to watch the BBC again. It was all day and night, and I started making friends who couldn't speak Urdu, so I couldn't just take the easy road.

When I came to Canada, I had three job interviews and received three job offers. It was just amazing. At my interview with Kellogg's, I sat there and thought about what I had learned about the North American way of talking. I knew in our culture it was not a good thing to boast about yourself and appear to be too confident and not humble. So I said in the interview, "Look, I am coming from a different background, so it is very difficult for me when you ask me the question, 'Hassan, can you do that?' The cultural conditioning for me is to say, 'I will try to do that.'" The English that I spoke was a little different, and people didn't understand my accent when I came to Canada for the first time. Again, I put myself to the test of making sure that I improved myself.

I don't think there was such a huge shock in the transition from Canada to the US; my immediate reaction was that it looked the same. The buildings, the roads, even the shops. It was the same KFC, the same McDonald's. But, of course there are differences. Canada is very laid back, and Americans are more active in taking initiative. Canada is culturally more "thinking through, taking time, and then taking action." In the US it is more just "action."

It was not just three cultures that I had been exposed to during this time. I have actually travelled to more than sixty countries at this point, and I have met people from all over the world. It is very interesting to see how human beings are different yet similar, and there are some really interesting stories all around.

Starting a company was never my dream. Even today, that is not really the driver. From the very beginning, my childhood and upbringing were pretty much like American thinking: you can do whatever you like in your life. That is not the norm in Pakistan. My parents gave me that opportunity and it was really, really good. I always had a problem with understanding everything that was going on, always asking the question, "Why?" That got me in a lot of problems, by the way, but I never stopped asking. With the "Why" comes understanding, and then that leads to, "Okay, how can I improve it?" I wasn't always like that; I used to break things a lot. All my toys were broken; my dad would bring toys and I would just unscrew them and take them apart. He sometimes got very upset and would say, "Hassan, it is not going to break like that. Let me bring a hammer, you can smash it with a hammer easier." So that is how it was.

When I started Zentech Corporation, which was an ERP software company in Canada, I thought about my past experiences. I used to work for a paint manufacturing company, and when I came to Canada, I was still thinking about the manufacturing process in the paint industry at that time. ERP was just beginning, and I thought that this was a great opportunity to bring something better to that industry. That is how I started thinking about Zentech Corporation.

When I came to the US, my first job was at this nonprofit organization called Speeches 360. Once I finished designing software intended for zoos all over the world, I was curious; I thought, "Okay, maybe I should now go and see how zoos really work." Of course I learned a lot. I joined a zoo as executive director in the UK and worked there for a year and a half. That was another culture shock.

I thought about how ideas go into action. I reached out to fifty friends and asked, "Would you want to help me with this?" They said yes. I think it was not like, "I am going to start a company." It was like, "What do people do when they have an idea, and how do they work on those ideas so that curiosity leads them to think about why something is the way it is? And then how do you change something for the better?" I think that is my driver. I think the first basic thing that drives me is figuring out how to help people.

Of course, there are challenges being an immigrant. The biggest one is that you don't have those deep-rooted networks that you build when you are a kid, when you are in school, when you are in university. You are building relationships that are for life, but then you come to a country where you don't know anybody. I literally landed in Canada and did not know anyone. In Bahrain, my sister was there and had a big circle of friends. In Canada I did not know whether to turn right or left from the airport. I knew where I was going to stay, but that was pretty much it. There was no Internet at that time to tell you which hotel to go to or where to stay.

I came to the US for a job, so I knew a few people that I had met before. But it was not like I had a friend circle or a family over here. I think this is the biggest problem: people tend to gravitate to the people that they can relate to, and in an immigrant community it is hard to build those connections. I think this is especially difficult when you are looking to start a company and thinking about the sales process. In the Industrial Age sales process, you could see that I am selling this glass, for example. But in a knowledge-based business, you cannot point to an object and tell a customer, "This is what I am selling." Without having those alliances, without having those networks, it becomes really difficult to get your first few success stories. I think that is something that is difficult for entrepreneurs in Minnesota, and for immigrant entrepreneurs it is even more difficult because they don't get even that initial support.

Life is all about learning, and there are lots of things that you learn when you start a business. I think the biggest thing for anybody who is starting a business is to think of what propels them. The common thinking of, "I will start a business, I am my own boss," or, "I am going to make a lot of money," has nothing to do with an immigrant entrepreneur. Entrepreneurship is a constant dance between success and failure. You can't maintain that unless you have something that is driving you; otherwise you will very quickly get bogged down by the failures and the roadblocks you are facing. When you are working at a job, you can go to your boss for help. When you are an entrepreneur, you can't go to anyone; you have to have that internal drive. I think that is the learning process, and it is still a learning process—I am not through with it. I feel this is important to share with everybody who is thinking about starting a business.

All three of my kids were born in Canada. I came to Canada and my first daughter was born; then we had a son and another daughter. When we came to the US, they were all young—our youngest was one year old. They are all big now and can take care of themselves; I don't need to worry about them. I think that is a natural progression in your life—even if I were living somewhere else, I would go through that. Now that the kids are grown up, life is a lot simpler. I think the biggest challenge right now for me is the cost of their college. My daughter just finished her degree. She was the first woman of color at her university to be elected student body president. I think that that is really good for her and for the other students to see what can be done in Minnesota; to see that there is an opportunity for immigrants to go that far.

Now most of my time is spent on my work. I wake up at five o'clock in the morning and I go to bed at ten. Pretty much all that time is work. During the weekends we try to do family activities, as my daughter comes home on weekends. We play some games or watch TV or movies, things like that, American things that the American families would do. There is nothing very exciting about it, but having that family time is important and gives you a leg up as an entrepreneur. It is more healing, you know, to sit with your family and talk about stuff.

My current company, Ideagist, started with the question, "What do people do when they get frustrated with something?" Of course, the gift of entrepreneurship is that you start with something, and then you learn and improve, which leds to a more fundamental question, "What do people do when they come up with an idea?" When you ask this question to individuals, you get a range of answers. A majority of them say, "I don't know what to do." When you're in a company and you have an idea, there is a process. But when you are starting with your own idea, you really don't know what to do, and that was the reason why we moved Ideagist to where it is now.

Ideagist is a virtual incubator for people with early-stage ideas, the beginnings. The whole world is going to get behind you when you have something interesting to show. But when you don't have something to show and it's just an idea, there is very little help that you can get. That is where we would like to make a difference. When we started, people used to say, "What do you do? Why is it important? I can learn this anywhere. With the Internet, everything is available." But then when we started building our process and people started seeing the outcome.

Last year we started a cohort where anybody from anywhere in the world could pitch a start-up idea to the group. If the idea was accepted, we gave the person mentors and a process to work through it. In January 2018, we had 200 people in our first cohort. That is unimaginable for any of the incubation environments you could think of—for most incubators and excubators, the cohort size is twenty to forty, max. We are scaling it up to a level that has never been done before. We are currently hosting more than 2,000 ideas. If you took one of the top incubators or excubators in the US, they might have only helped 2,000 ideas in their whole lifetime. The scale at which we now help people through Ideagist is just amazing and that is what is exciting.

I think that the biggest thing so far in the US that I was able to contribute was my first job, which was helping to build a system that is now used by more than a thousand zoos all over the world. The biggest contribution was not the technology or the software that was built, but the collaboration that was created by bringing people together and agreeing on data standards that they now use to share knowledge among themselves. The software can change, new versions can come out, but those collaborations that were established—the people who work together and agree on those data standards, who went to conferences and workshops together—those relationships are for life.

I hope that is the contribution they are seeing, that they will continue to make those relationships, and that those standards that they have developed will continue to bring more benefits in terms of knowledge—learning about the animals, how we are keeping them, and how we are treating them.

MEDIA LINKS

greencardvoices.org/speakers/hassan-syed

Yaoundé,
Cameroon

Veronica Quillien

Born: Madison, Wisconsin
Rasied: Yaoundé, Cameroon
Current City: Minneapolis, MN

Current Business:
Language Attitude
languageattitude.org

> "THE THREE CORNERSTONES OF REMAKING MY CULTURAL IDENTITY WERE HOW I DANCED, HOW I WORE MY HAIR, AND HOW I SPOKE."

My father was one of three bright Cameroonian scholars who received funding through the United States Agency for International Development to pursue their educations at American universities. My father attended the University of Wisconsin in Madison. I was born in Madison; that's where life began for me. My family returned to Cameroon after my parents completed their education.

In the '80s, my siblings and I visited my father's family in Cameroon. In the '90s, we visited my mother's family. Both places were very familial. My maternal grandfather taught us a song, "Enfants de la même cité," and we sang it every night before we went to bed. We sang it together one last time at his funeral in 2010.

During summer vacation, there were at minimum twenty grandchildren running around; you can imagine the commotion. We entertained ourselves. We practiced swimming in the river. The girls learned how to braid by practicing on each other's hair. We were always encouraged to eat fruit, until we over-consumed it. One of my funniest memories is climbing on mango trees and eating mangoes all day. We quickly learned that eating too many mangoes gives you diarrhea.

During the school year in the city, family members visited all the time. We lived in a multigenerational household, including my great-grandmother. I was my great-grandmother's shadow. She's my namesake. I called her Mbombo. One of the things we loved to do together was to work the land. When I was working the land with her, she said, "You can cultivate whatever you want." So I cultivated only peanuts.

She taught me how to make peanut butter from scratch. We first grilled the peanuts, then ground them. When Mbombo made peanut butter for herself, she didn't add sugar. When she made it for me, she did. I liked to boil my harvested peanuts. She taught me how to separate my boiled peanuts into different-sized containers and sell them. The one thing Mbombo wanted to instill in me was independence through interdependence. Mbombo said, in our language: "This, you can sell it for this much, this, you can sell it for this much."

After I came back from selling my boiled peanuts, I had pocket money. I learned to count through this practice; I was still bad at math, though. Selling my boiled peanuts was my first enterprise. I had a simple goal: to get money to buy sweets. I had a particular chocolate bar that I liked. At that age, less than ten years old, it was the thing only that I wanted to buy.

I was bored in school. I wasn't motivated enough, or maybe I was just learning differently. Dance and music mattered to me. For example, when Mbombo's favorite song played on the radio, she asked me to come and dance for her, and at the end of the dance she gave me money. So dancing and music were very much part of me, of what I did growing up, because that's how we got money from elders.

Then, on October 10, 1994, we moved to Côte d'Ivoire. I remember that day clearly because it was the most intense pain I had ever felt as a child. Leaving was very painful, because I was leaving everything that I loved, everything that I knew, and the people who cared about me for another life. I was debating with myself, trying to figure out, "Okay, what's going to happen?" I thought, "Okay, it's just Africa, it's not going to be that bad, right? It's not going to be that bad; it's going to be okay. People are going to look like me." And I got there and it was very brutal in the sense that it was a completely different lifestyle from what I was used to. For example: Hair was worn very differently in Côte d'Ivoire. My hair was natural. After my first week in school, I begged my mom to perm my hair so I could look like everybody else.

The language was also very different. Although we spoke French, it was a different French because of the intonation and the rhythm. Everything that makes up a language was very different. I was lost, completely lost, and for that first academic year, I kept promising myself that by the end of the school year I was going to speak and behave like an Ivorian. I spent time strategizing how to belong, like everybody else. By the end of that school year in '95, I spoke and behaved like an Ivorian. The three cornerstones of remaking my cultural identity were how I danced, how I wore my hair, and how I spoke.

I learned from an early age to strategize around a particular situation.

As an adult now, I am more sophisticated in my strategic planning. Because we moved frequently when I was growing up, I developed a high level of adaptability by assessing a given situation and strategizing responses very quickly.

I figured out strategies to deal with leaving people behind. At the time, we had email, but it wasn't as prominent as it is now, so before leaving it was important to have everyone's postal addresses. We wrote handwritten letters. I still love handwritten letters. I still send them. Phone numbers, too, were very, very important. Those were the tools to communicate.

When war broke out in Côte d'Ivoire, my mother told us that we were going on a vacation in Belgium to visit my uncle. We went there and never, never came back. That was a bummer. But, by that time in my life, it was much easier to leave because I had learned earlier in life to deal with separation.

Because we had attended a French school in Côte d'Ivoire, my parents decided that it was easier to continue in a French system. It was important for my parents that the children stay together, so my mother found a school that could take all of us in Armentières, France. During the week we were in boarding school; on the weekend we returned to Brussels. There was a lot of back and forth. Every Friday, my siblings and I packed our suitcases for Brussels. Every Sunday, my siblings and I packed our suitcases for Armentières. Every Monday, we got up at four in the morning. We went to the train station and got on the train to be at school at eight. It was very strenuous for young kids. My sister was nine.

One day, we all slept on the train and traveled into the Flemish part of Belgium. We knew nothing about Flemish. It was scary because everybody was white and we were four black kids who did not understand a word of the language. Our survival skills kicked in and we quickly became aware of our surroundings. We jumped off the running train and carefully walked onto the other ramp. We got into the next train to recross the border. That day, of course, we were late to school. From then on, we established a system to make sure it never happened again. Now we laugh when we talk about it in the family. At the time, it was frightening and very painful.

Confidence was important growing up. Now, if we couldn't figure out how to fix a problem, we had to explain why we brought it up. We were raised to find solutions to the problems we faced in life. Assurance was also a big part of growing up. It was very important to talk with assurance. Given our highly mobile life, letting out an ounce of doubt could be life threatening. Being unsure of a situation could leave us vulnerable. My siblings and I developed those skills very early on.

In France, I was in the equivalent of the twelfth grade here in the US. To graduate from high school, everyone took the baccalauréat, which is the national exam in the francophone school system. I passed the test; after that it was college. College in my family meant returning to the US, because we were American citizens, born here. Receiving financial aid would reduce the family financial burden. After graduation, I jumped on a plane and landed in Chicago. I spent the summer in Racine, a suburb of Milwaukee, because my brother was doing an internship there. Then I landed in Superior, Wisconsin. That was a big shock. I had never seen so many white people per square mile. I lived in cosmopolitan places. And even a small town like Armentières had a mix of everybody. In Superior, it was just white. Plain white. I couldn't eat the food. I couldn't find clothes that fit. Everything was just bad. And then I had to learn English. I had to go to class, do all these things that were expected of me, yet I'd never been prepared for life in rural America. I had to make the best out of it.

In 2001, at the University of Superior–Wisconsin, there were five African students on campus. I really didn't care about making friends at that time, because I was on a mission: finish school and get out. So my friends were literally my brother and his friends. They were all my older brothers.

I graduated in three years because I just wanted to get out of there. I was not yet twenty-one, so there was really no nightlife for me. I managed to study abroad in France until I turned twenty-one. When I returned, I could actually enjoy the nightlife. That made a difference for me, but my stomach had still not adjusted to the food. To this day, I am very particular with the food that I eat. I can't eat just anything because my stomach is very sensitive.

I received a Pell Grant, so I did a work-study program on campus. I worked at the cafeteria and the radio station. I really, really loved the radio station work because it was one way for me to express myself and talk about those identities that I had. My hosting name on the radio was "The French Chick," because France was the closest reference. My first job off campus was at Dairy Queen. I worked there for maybe a year and a half. Then, I was a teller at US Bank, and that got me through finishing college. I arrived in Superior in 2001. Fast forward to 2006, and I got my first job after graduating, at Lake Superior College.

In 2006, I was appointed the director of intercultural services at Lake Superior College. In that position, I realized I did not understand the American educational system because I had a different history and no understanding of the historical determinants necessary to navigate the system. Having a good grasp of the American educational system was very important. To understand the system, I worked my way up from early childhood education. I taught early childhood. Then, I held a different position within the K–12 system.

As a K–12 educator, I identified opportunities to develop services beyond my assigned duties. I incorporated the Metamorphosis Project in Duluth, MN. The program was offered from 2011 to 2016. We began by creating a space to build black girls' assets and nurture their positive outlook on life. By the end, we built robots with elementary students. Over those five years, the program experienced a metamorphosis in the services we provided.

I retired the nonprofit after I began my doctoral program at the University of Minnesota. After analyzing my new environment, I partook in several entrepreneurial programs available at the university such as the Acara Challenge. I realized that there was so much that I could do for my research with the resources available at the University of Minnesota.

As a doctoral student, what mattered to me was relearning my language. I shared my transformation in Côte d'Ivoire and the survival skills I subsequently developed. Now, my life purpose is to research who I am by learning about my culture and language. Initially, that meant going home and reconnecting with family members that I hadn't seen since the '90s. Researching also meant I had to, again, strategize on how to gather the resources I needed.

From there, one thing led to another and I got to a point where I said, "You know what? I'm going to do this." I gathered my money and incorporated Language Attitude in the 2016 fall semester. Language Attitude is a research-driven corporation that offers research-based solutions to communities affected by culture and language loss. We revitalize language by promoting and protecting oral traditions with youth on science experiments. We create an interconnected spiderweb. Our foundation is grounded in a traditional Bàsàa knowledge system. From there, we reimagine with art to remake our culture.

I began researching traditional Bàsàa storytelling techniques to conceptualize a pedagogy and to design Vac'Art, the summer language and art camp that takes place in Cameroon every other year. Youths attending the camp in summer 2018 will curate and launch the first Bàsàa traveling oral tradition museum. The traveling museum will contain animations, books, ceramics, and a musical. To conceptualize this traveling museum, I collaborated with artists and elders based in Cameroon and Minnesota to modernize oral tradition.

To develop my entrepreneurial spirit, I am always referring back to the skills and competence my parents instilled in me. As part of his scholarly research, my dad developed this simple model: assess the problem, figure out different options, pick the option to apply. Evaluate it and figure out if it works or not.

I wouldn't be here without my parents or my grandparents, who sacrificed even more for my parents to have a higher level of education and seek better opportunities for us. My research allows me, through Language Attitude, to promote and protect our indigenous methodologies back to my communities in Cameroon and Minnesota.

The skills I developed along the way—such as being highly adaptable, knowing and understanding the system within which I work, and strategizing to access those resources—come from the opportunities my parents afforded me. At the University of Minnesota, different funding has leveraged the resources to advance my research agenda. I was a recipient of multiple fellowships such as the US Department Foreign Language and Area Studies Fellowship, the International Perspective on International Development, and the Graduate School Summer Research Internship. At a community level, I was selected to be part of the Change Network Minnesota, an initiative of the Bush Foundation.

Connecting with people who enhance my skills and understand how I work is the reason I've been very successful with the language and art camp in Cameroon, in collaboration with our affiliate association, RESTART. Lessons and failures are my big motivators.

I'm graduating next year, so I am preparing for the next step in life as a Change Network Minnesota fellow. My goal, through Language Attitude, is to make research-based products accessible to my community in Cameroon and Minnesota. As part of that fellowship, I am networking to launch the ArtiVist Research Group (ARG), a social enterprise owned and operated by Language Attitude. ARG will promote sustainable agriculture with farmers in southern Cameroon to manage their natural resources. Language Attitude is interested in changes that benefit communities. Reciprocity and relationality are part of our work. Through our research, we ensure that science listens to, acknowledges, and benefits indigenous communities.

As a PhD candidate at the University of Minnesota, I work as a research assistant on international initiatives within the College of Food, Agriculture, and Natural Science Resources and the College of Design. When I'm not entrepreneuring or when I'm not a student, I like to be home and watch a TV series or a movie—especially action movies, because I grew up in the '90s with Jackie Chan, Sylvester Stallone, Van Damme, and the like. I love dance and music shows such as *Dancing with the Stars* or *The Voice*. Of course this is not to forget *Scandal* or *Being Mary Jane*, shows portraying empowered black women.

I love to hang out with my friends. I have to admit, having friends is a muscle I am relearning to stretch. Growing up highly mobile, making friends was as painful as leaving them behind because I did not know when the next move would be. Agreeing to be part of Green Card Voices' entrepreneur book is sharing who I am, the struggles and opportunities that lie between the pain and joy.

What has really shifted for me is understanding how to talk about painful events with a positive light, and for me, art has really been the tool that I've used to do that. What my parents taught me is my guiding principle: I cannot sit and complain about things. I must come up with solutions. What's the solution to this problem? And if I cannot find the solution, then I need to stop complaining. This outlook has really shifted who I am, especially since I started my doctoral program in 2014–researching back and re-centering myself, knowing where I came from and what matters to me, and naming the lifelong skills that have brought me to where I am.

I am grateful for my parents, for giving us and for affording us this world. There is a lot that they had to give up for us to be here, and being here is their return on investment.

MEDIA LINKS

greencardvoices.org/speakers/veronica-quillien

Chatham,
Canada

Vikas Narula

From: Chatham, Canada
Current City: Minneapolis, MN

Current Business:
Keyhubs
keyhubs.com

> "WHAT IS WHISPERING AND TUGGING AT YOUR HEART?. . . ARE YOU ACTING ON IT?
> MAYBE IT LEADS TO ENTREPRENEURSHIP, MAYBE IT DOESN'T. BUT WHEREVER IT LEADS,
> IT'S GOING TO TAKE YOU ON A JOURNEY OF GROWTH AND LEARNING AND ADVENTURE."

My parents immigrated from India to Canada in the late '60s. We lived in a small town in southern Ontario. My father was a high school teacher, and I had one older brother. It was a very good place to grow up.

When I was eleven, I was informed we were moving to the United States. My parents were very avid followers of Maharishi Mahesh Yogi, who brought Transcendental Meditation to the West—he had started a school, a community, and a university in Fairfield, Iowa. When my parents heard about this community, they were very eager to move there and to have my brother and me enroll in the school.

I remember the journey quite clearly. We took a train from Chatham, Ontario, to Mount Pleasant, Iowa, which is about thirty miles east of Fairfield. It was late August, and we arrived in Iowa with a lot of anticipation and excitement. When we got off at the train station, for whatever reason our ride did not show up, and so we waited there. At the time it was just my mother, my brother, and I, and we had a bunch of luggage.

We didn't have cell phones back then, and we didn't know anyone in Fairfield at that time. My mom improvised—we walked a few blocks away from the train station, where there was a family out in the yard. They could tell we were lost or looking for help, and said, "Where are you guys going? Do you guys need help?" My mom explained to them that we were trying to get to Fairfield and our ride hadn't shown up. They said, "Oh, that's no problem, we'll take you."

So we just loaded up in their car, and these people we didn't even know drove us to Fairfield. They wouldn't take any money for gas or anything. They showed us around the town a little bit. What a great way to come to the United States. I think it was very telling of the spirit here.

For me, the biggest challenge of coming to the United States at eleven was giving up my life, especially the friends who I'd grown up with in Canada since I could remember. Hockey is a big part of life in Canada, especially for an eleven-year-old boy. We watched and played hockey year round—on the ice and or on the street. I knew that in Fairfield, Iowa, there wasn't going to be any hockey. That was the hardest part of coming to America. But the community, the new friends I made, and the new experiences certainly made up for the absence of hockey in my life.

I completed sixth–twelfth grade at the Maharishi School, which was a very enriching experience. It was certainly not the mainstream educational experience that one has in America or elsewhere, because we had yoga and meditation integrated into our curriculum. It shaped my own philosophy around life, creating a foundation. The community there in Fairfield, Iowa, was very nurturing; it was a great place to grow up.

After I graduated from high school, I enrolled at the Maharishi University and studied computer science. I graduated in '94 and joined a start-up company called Vital Images, founded by a professor at the university. They were doing some very interesting, cutting-edge 3-D imaging. Shortly after I joined that company, they were acquired by a medical device company in the Twin Cities. When I was twenty-four, they opened an office in Minneapolis, and I moved up there. I had lived in Fairfield for thirteen years; that was quite a bit of time to be in a small town, and I was ready to spread my wings. Of course, no shortage of hockey here in Minneapolis!

Shortly after moving, I met my wife, Priya. We got married when I was twenty-six. Six years later we had our first child. We have two boys, born in 2003 and 2007. I spent the first eleven years of my career working for Vital Images. It did very well for itself, and working there was a great experience. I traveled the world, and then I switched jobs and joined another start-up company in the same industry—the radiology industry. The name of that company was Virtual Radiologic. It also did very well for itself—it was a start-up, fast-growth company. That was a great experience.

The two founders who I worked for certainly influenced me. I was inspired by them, their passion for their ideas, and their commitment to their customers. Later on, when I quit my job and became an entrepreneur myself, I was looking for other really successful entrepreneurs who I wanted to emulate, who inspired me and did things that were very out of the ordinary. Tony Shay comes to mind; I thought the way he built a business on creating a culture around customer service was really courageous and different. I was really inspired by videos I found about people who reinvented themselves, who were doing one thing before deciding to shred it all and go do some other thing that ended up being really successful.

While I was at Virtual Radiologic, I decided to get my MBA. It was while pursuing this that I got an idea for a business, Keyhubs, which started as a hobby back in 2007 and slowly evolved. I ended up quitting my job to pursue Keyhubs full time in 2009. That's what I've been working on since, and it's been a wonderful experience being an entrepreneur.

I think I've always had entrepreneurial tendencies. I like to create new things, and used to be in science fairs when I was younger. The thing I enjoyed most about science fairs was the showmanship and presentation. I had that kind of outgoing, sales-like approach to things. From a young age I liked to start clubs. These are all entrepreneurial tendencies.

When I worked for various start-ups, I got to see how a business gets going, launches its products, and makes some profit. But I never really thought that I would start my own business until much later, when I went to school and learned about different types of businesses and case studies. What I was drawn to were the case studies and businesses that were more entrepreneurial, and I saw that some of my tendencies were on the start-up side of things. While I was at school, I got an idea for a business, and I had this epiphany that maybe I should be an entrepreneur.

As an entrepreneur, I feel very fortunate to be living and working in a country that is, in a sense, a beacon of light for innovation. I didn't appreciate this growing up—when you look at America, it's a very young, start-up-like country, but it's also the oldest modern democracy. It's a pioneer in the free-market system. Many of the companies that are changing the world started here. On top of that, we have this incredible diversity. There's beauty everywhere in the world: beautiful people and rich cultures. I think what separates America from the rest is that all of these different people and cultures live together in relative peace and harmony. I don't think you can find that anywhere else in the world. I feel very fortunate and very proud to live in the United States of America.

I don't know what it's like not to be an immigrant entrepreneur, so I don't know if it would've been easier or harder to take a different path. In some ways I've been given more opportunities because of how I stand out—I'm a minority. I think that our systems are set up so that people want to see more minorities at work. America is a country where there is a push toward the value of diversity and inclusion. People see that I am not from here, that my family comes from Asia, and maybe they want to give me more of a chance, though it's hard to say. I think entrepreneurship is hard, period. That transcends whether you're an immigrant or not.

I think what's helped me as an immigrant entrepreneur is that I don't sell only to people who look like me or who are from my background. I like to think of myself as a bridge between different groups and backgrounds. There is research that says this puts you in an advantageous position, both for your personal perspective and your career. I like to think part of my success comes from being able to relate to a lot of clients.

One of the things that I'm most proud about in my life, specifically my life here in America, is my involvement in planting trees and giving trees to schoolkids. This was a project that I got involved with in my college days in Iowa. Over a few years, we raised money and gave away tens of thousands of small trees for kids to plant on Earth Day. That's probably one of the most gratifying things I've done in my life—it was a very selfless, giving activity. I got to see the smiling faces of these kids getting trees. I tracked a lot of the trees that we planted, and twenty years later, they're humongous. They're beautifying our communities. I've done a lot of things and contributed in different ways, but that's something that sticks out in my mind because those trees are probably going to outlive me.

I've learned so much, and I give whatever I can give. The entrepreneurial journey really changed my life for the better in so many ways. I stumbled into entrepreneurship because I had these quiet whispers in my heart, saying maybe I should do this thing or create that thing. I didn't know how it would turn out, I just went with it.

What is whispering and tugging at your heart? Are you listening to it? Are you acting on it? Maybe it leads to entrepreneurship, maybe it doesn't. But wherever it leads, it's going to take you on a journey of growth and learning and adventure. And I think that is what life is about: the feeling of being alive. It's not easy; there are a lot of ups and downs. It doesn't go as planned, but I wouldn't trade it for anything. It's about creating, it's about sharing your creation, it's about learning as you go. It's a surprise of positive and negative, of turning the negative *into* positive, of seeing good in all things. Life itself is an entrepreneurial journey. And my journey happens to include entrepreneurship in the professional domain as well as the personal.

I got here with help from God and lots of people, and of course with a lot of timing and hard work. I couldn't have done it by myself. It has been a wonderful journey, one I've been very fortunate to live through. I've gotten to experience small town, rural American life; I've gotten to live in a community that was off the beaten path and focused on more than just things of a material nature; and now I've gotten to enjoy life in the big city and been exposed to so many different types of people and industries. I'm very grateful.

MEDIA LINKS

greencardvoices.org/speakers/vikas-narula

Kingston,
Jamaica

Tomme Beevas

From: Kingston, Jamaica
Current City: Minneapolis, MN

Current Business:
Pimento Jamaican Kitchen
pimentokitchen.com

> "I WOULD LEAVE MY SIXTY-HOUR, SIX-FIGURE JOB AS AN EXECUTIVE, GO HOME, AND FIRE UP THE GRILL, TRYING TO CONNECT WITH MY CULTURE AS WELL AS DE-STRESS; WHO DOESN'T LOVE COOKING?"

My life in Jamaica was awesome. Essentially, I had the best of all worlds. I lived in uptown Kingston, which was a wealthier part of town, but my family's heritage stems from the heart of Bob Marley's west Kingston. I had the pleasure of being both uptown and downtown, hanging out with the rich kids and the ruffians. Kingston is a microcosm of the world. There are so many tourists throughout the island, but Kingston is only for those who are truly brave, who are ready to come visit the New York of Jamaica. It is the spiritual capital of the country, it's the financial capital of the country, and it's the political capital of the country.

Being there in the heart of Jamaica, in the heart of Kingston, you never missed anything: We had the best food on the island, in my opinion. Not the best beaches, but good-enough beaches. The people were a very eclectic group—there were people who were traveling around the world, or people who were from the countryside coming into the big city for the first time. I was able to interact with so many different perspectives. I think that really colored my view of the world, teaching me that it is much larger than the self. Moving to the United States was a tricky situation. It started with this beautiful scar on my body. Back in Kingston, while studying at the University of West Indies, I was attacked on campus. At that point, my family and I had two thoughts: one, that it was difficult for me to get into the university itself because I was doing pre-university work there, and two, based on the risk, I might as well go seek opportunities elsewhere.

So I packed up and moved to Miami. This was around the time Will Smith released "Miami," so I was excited. I decided that I was going to pack up with just one suitcase. I don't even know if I had money, but nevertheless, I figured it out. I had two aunts there; I started sleeping on one aunt's couch and then got my own apartment. Within a few months, I was really involved in the Miami community as a student. After that I ended up moving to Tampa, where I finished up at the University of South Florida with my economics and political science degrees.

Of course, there weren't many opportunities for politics and economics in Florida, so I got recruited to go to Washington, DC, where I worked at the US Chamber of Commerce and did some work for the White House on the president's Volunteer Service Award. Eventually, I got recruited out of DC to move to the wonderful state of Minnesota, where I started off as director of community development for a food company. I had the pleasure of working in probably sixty countries on global community relations issues. Whether it was hunger in the horn of Africa or environmental issues in Indonesia, I was able to see the world from right here in Minnesota.

Naturally, one has to give up a lot in order to become an American. Let's start with our communication: I had to quickly switch from speaking in a Jamaican patois to sounding as Minnesotan as possible so I wouldn't stick out too much. That's one of the things even English-speaking immigrants have to face—figuring out how to "speak American." The other sacrifice is your food and, along with that, the people you're familiar with. This created an opportunity for me. I would go home from my wonderful corporate job every day missing home, and I'd fire up the grill and cook some Jamaican jerk chicken to connect with the place I'd left.

Moving to Florida wasn't that much of a culture shock, thankfully, because ever since I was five years old I'd traveled back and forth from Kingston to Miami. I summered in New York. I had family living in Massachusetts, including my mom and dad, so I was quite familiar with American culture. Moving to Miami was still a bit different, though, because I had to figure out how to survive and thrive, living permanently in this country, while also starting college. It was definitely a culture shock trying to settle in—managing all the facets of being a college student, trying to figure out how to be an independent man and an immigrant in America—but thankfully Miami is such a melting pot; it was a much more welcoming community than others I could have moved to. Everybody around was an immigrant too. Everybody was trying to figure these things out.

I wouldn't say I was always an entrepreneur—and yet, in third grade, I had more lunch money than the other kids, and I would lend them money with a high interest rate. That was perhaps my first taste of being an entrepreneur.

My family has always been entrepreneurial. I'm now the third generation to have created a million-dollar company. My parents and grandparents have been my entrepreneurial role models—I've seen them coming from the heart of a Jamaican ghetto to build their own empires. That, of course, inspired me to build my own.

The opportunity to become an entrepreneur came to me while I was still working in corporate America. I would leave my sixty-hour, six-figure job as an executive, go home, and fire up the grill, trying to connect with my culture as well as de-stress; Who doesn't love cooking? My neighbors smelled the food, and then we literally took my grill and a hundred-dollar tent from Target and brought them out onto the streets of Minneapolis. This was the beginning of Pimento Jamaican Kitchen, which is something of an homage to my grandmother, from whom I learned to cook.

Pimento Jamaican Kitchen is definitely a grassroots movement. It started with people saying, "You know, I love Jamaican food, but here's how we can do it differently." For example, our jerk chicken is boneless, even though you'd never find a boneless chicken running around Jamaica. We had to learn how Minnesotans and Americans appreciate the food and figure out how to keep it authentic yet flexible.

Our very first event was the Bryn Mawr garage sale in my neighborhood, where I gave away the food free in exchange for feedback—we literally had a full survey—and following our social media. From there, we started doing other street events with my business partner, Yoni, who's also my neighbor. We took my grill and our tent and went around to local street events—art events for our first year—to figure out how it worked.

Fast-forward: we got cast for, and won, a Food Network reality show, Food Court Wars, which gave us our own location at the Burnsville Center free for a year. That was an amazing opportunity—we had start-up capital and a low-risk environment to test the recipes and the concept. I'd never worked in a restaurant, not even flipping burgers or serving—I learned everything through our experience with Pimento—and it was a blessing to have that Food Network reality show give us our own space so we could test it.

Fast-forward further, and I was basically doing both my corporate job and the restaurant at the same time. Sixty hours over there, forty hours over there, every single week. A year later, after the model was proven, I felt confident and comfortable enough to step away from my corporate job to help grow the business. That's where we are right now; we're at our third location, ready to open up our fourth. We also have our food truck, and we're opening a Jamaican rum bar! We have an amazing patio. The goal is to create

Little Jamaica right here in Minnesota, where you can come home, have a Red Stripe and some good jerk chicken, and don't worry, eat happy.

Being an immigrant entrepreneur doesn't come without issues. You're not used to the community where you're living, oftentimes you're not used to the language people are speaking, and the cultural approaches to American bureaucracy are a huge challenge for most immigrants. Thanks to my own hardships in the city of Minneapolis like trying to figure out the application process for things like liquor licenses, I'm now serving on the Innovation Committee for the city to help identify ways in which the process can be simplified for start-up businesses. I explained to them that for a Somali woman—let's call her Baby Lue, my grandmother's name—who's trying to start her own company, not speaking the language, not having an MBA or even a college education, and having to figure out the bureaucracy in America is extremely difficult. My goal with the Innovation Committee is to help figure out how to streamline the process, simplifying it to the point where Baby Lue from Somalia can take a one-page application and start a business here in Minnesota. It shouldn't be that difficult.

Becoming an entrepreneur is an identity crisis. You're coming from being a student, unemployed, or, in my case, a corporate executive, and learning to be your own person, creating your own brand and your company's brand. As immigrants, many of us simply don't have the resources that others have, people who have been able to hand down resources from generation to generation. We also don't have the same connections: "Oh, my uncle's father's cousin works here, there, and everywhere else." We have to start from zero in order to build our own enterprises here. But when entrepreneurs come to America and they learn about the American Dream, that they can truly become anything they want, that fire keeps them going. They say to themselves, "Look, if I'm gonna be here, I'm going to win." That's why immigrants tend to win so much in America.

My life in America today is interesting. I'm a Jamaican who has a child born in Edina, Minnesota. Just today we were snowed in and I needed to go shovel the sidewalk, and I said, "You know what? Let me take my daughter with me." So there I am with this fourteen-month-old in a snowsuit. A snowsuit! The first person in my entire family to wear a snowsuit is my little daughter. And there we are out on the sidewalk shoveling snow together. She's as Jamaican as they come—she loves herself some jerk chicken, even at fourteen months—but the fact that she's out there having fun in the snow shows that as a species we're very resilient. We're very adaptable.

The fact that I'm able to move from the tropics to the cold tundra—the Bold North, as we call it—to be selling jerk chicken on the streets of Minnesota in the snow, and at the same time having a child who says, "Hey, ain't a thing," frolicking in the snow, says to us that we should approach life like a one-year-old no matter what. Have fun, keep going, keep moving; when you fall, get right back up. It's that simple.

That brings me to my perspective on the current climate for immigrants in the US. It is one of hope, one of true belief, because America was invented by immigrants. We all came here to build, which is the great hope for so many people around the world. America is just naturally is a land of immigrants. The demographics show that it's shifting—the future is immigrant, the future is female, the future is black, the future is gay, the future is everything. The future in America is for all of us. That's what gives me hope, that's what keeps me going every day, building our empire so everybody else can enjoy that little piece of Jamaica here locally.

My former role was in corporate responsibility. I had the pleasure of addressing local issues across the United States or in three hundred cities around the world. One of the things I'm proudest of today is the brand Pimento Jamaican Kitchen and what we're doing in Minnesota: helping to break down stereotypes about Jamaica and immigrants; providing people a safe home to relax and enjoy and believe they're in Jamaica; breaking the average Minnesotan out of their "Minnesota Nice" and have them come to Jamaica. We want to be authentic, be fun, live well, be happy, stop worrying, and serve as an ambassador of Jamaica to Minnesota. It's really a great feeling, and one of the proudest things that I've accomplished so far, that I'm able to help represent my old home in my new home.

MEDIA LINKS

greencardvoices.org/speakers/tomme-beevas

Bukavu,
Democratic Republic
of the Congo

Batul Walji

From: Bukavu, Democratic Republic of the Congo
Current City: Maple Grove, MN

Current Business:
Star Banners
starbannersmn.com

> "I HAD GROWN UP WITH MY MOM, WHO WAS A SEAMSTRESS, AND MY DAD, WHO OWNED A FABRIC STORE. I DEFINITELY GREW UP IN A FAMILY OF BUSINESS AND I ALWAYS HAD THAT IN MIND."

I was born in Bukavu, Congo, but the only thing I remember from there is the civil war. When I was four, my uncle drove us overnight to Burundi, where my parents were. Burundi was a beautiful place. It was very calm until 1990, when the genocide happened in Rwanda, but by that time I had already left. I don't have any negative memories about Burundi; it was very peaceful, a very fun place to be.

I left Burundi for the United States in 1982 because I had an arranged marriage. My husband moved here in 1972 as a refugee from Uganda, and when we married, I moved here to Minnesota to be with him. The hard part was leaving my family behind; the journey from Burundi meant not knowing where I was going, not knowing anything about the new country or my new family. And of course there was the language barrier. We spoke French there, and here it was English. I did understand a little bit, but it was hard for me. The whole culture here was different.

I knew my husband, though; I had met him. He came to pick me up, which was a good thing. We stopped in England, then Switzerland, and then came to Minnesota. Of course there was excitement because I had always heard good things about America, but at the same time, there was anxiousness.

After arriving here, I stayed with my in-laws, and they were very, very supportive; I'm really glad for them. It was very different. Back home in Burundi—I still call it home—you could walk anywhere and you knew everybody because the city was so small. Here it was hard because we lived in the suburbs. I couldn't go anywhere; I didn't know how or who to talk to. Not knowing English was difficult. But slowly, slowly, watching Sesame Street, I learned the language.

Everybody was so welcoming. That part for me was easy; people were very nice. I used to work at Marshall's and another store that closed down. At Marshall's, people were very, very friendly. I didn't have problem there with people. It could be hard at home—in Burundi we had maids who did all our chores, but here everything was on me—doing the chores, ironing, and all the rest. But other than that, it was fun.

I had grown up with my mom, who was a seamstress, and my dad, who owned a fabric store. I definitely grew up in a family of business, and I always had that in mind. When I moved here, I also started sewing clothes for people because I wanted to do something. I'm not the person who likes to sit back and do nothing. My dad, of course, was my inspiration, and my mom taught me how to sew. That led to me starting my business, Star Banners.

When I started Star Banners in 1990, it was me and my husband. My husband would come and help me at night and I would work in the daytime. I had two small kids when I started, a five-year-old and a three-year-old. That was difficult for me—being a mother and having small kids. The kids would sleep at night in the van outside our store, because we used to work until two or three in the morning; then we took them to school the next day. It was a struggle, but we made it happen.

I would say to everybody, as I tell my kids, don't give up. The first day may not work, but just wake up the next morning and push a little harder. Don't ever give up on your dreams, even though there will be obstacles. There were so many days when I said to my husband, "Let's close down. I don't want to do this anymore." It felt too hard, dealing with the home, and kids, and financial issues, and things like that. Just push yourself, I tell my children, and don't let yourself down; just wake up every day and know there is a new sun rising.

I've always been passionate about fashion design as well. I've launched a new website called Hijab Shack. I also have Mokka Fashion on Facebook, which I started to see where it could lead me. I'm so glad that Hijab Shack is growing, bringing new designs; we're always working on that.

As an entrepreneur, I believe that anybody who starts from scratch will have some kind of struggle. It doesn't matter where you are from. Struggles are going to be there: one day it will go well and another day you'll fall down, and you'll just have to get up and push yourself harder. As an immigrant, I could say, "Oh, it's harder for me." But I'm pretty sure it's hard for everybody who starts a business from scratch.

I give back to the community by hiring people and creating jobs and opportunities. I've always made it a point to hire other immigrants, specifically women, who may not have other opportunities for employment. I have also enlisted the help of youths in our community in order to help them continue their higher education. The reason I find this important is because I've always wanted to continue school, which I couldn't do back home. I keep telling my children they must go back to school. I also love helping, so I give my time to Feed My Starving Children or soup kitchens. In my spare time, I also enjoy crocheting and gardening.

I'm also a family person, and I have all my kids at home. That's something I enjoy. I have a granddaughter who is six months old, so I tell my kids, "Now you know how it feels to let go of your child." My kids are home, and they are everything to me.

MEDIA LINKS

greencardvoices.org/speakers/batul-walji

Salayea,
Liberia

Amara Kamara

From: Salayea, Liberia
Current City: Minneapolis, MN

Current Business:
Pillars Athletics Training
pillarstraining.com

> "DON'T HAVE A WAVERING MIND. STOP CONSIDERING EVERYTHING—FOCUS."

My name is Amara Solomon Kamara. I was named after my grandfather, who I have a lot of respect for. My grandfather had this belief that if I was named after him, I would carry a little soul of him, so I would have to take him with me. People know him as a Mandingo warrior. He was the first to put down a stone in the village where I was born, so they named the town after him too. My grandfather's name was Salayea, and that was the name of the town. My tribe is Mandinka, which is 99 percent Muslim.

I grew up with my grandfather in the village, but all my siblings lived in the capital city, Monrovia, and unlike me, they all went to school. My grandfather believed that if I went to school, Western education would totally change my behavior toward my own people and toward him, and I wouldn't be able to see what he had done for me. He said, "You can take everybody else. As long as this guy is named after me, he carries the soul of me—for that matter I'm going to keep him."

One night, when I was eleven, my mom came and woke me up. I felt like I was in a dream, but it was reality. She put me in the back of a big old truck and transported me to the capital city because she wanted me to go to school. And that's where my life started from.

My father had another woman. He had two wives, and these two women were so friendly. A lot of time people believe that when you have two wives they are going to fight all the time, but my parents were never like that. People couldn't tell whose mother was whose because the two women were so nice and friendly to each other. Before my father married my stepmother, my mother had to go to my stepmother's parents and beg them because they refused—they didn't want a marriage between two different dialects. At that time, people in different dialect groups marrying each other wasn't very popular, even though it was the same tribe.

My mother went there, lay on their floor, and begged them. "Please—allow my husband to marry your daughter. He's a good man." And they said that, if my mother was doing this, she would take good care of their daughter.

The one time they ever had a fight was because my mother is so humble and easygoing and my stepmother wouldn't go for it. When my dad did something wrong, she wanted to correct him. My mother wouldn't support my stepmother in trying to stop his behavior.

I had all of my siblings there—there are about eighteen of us from the same father, and we all have different mothers. Then my father married a Gola woman, whom he had one child with.

I started school when I was twelve years old, and they put me in kindergarten. I spent two weeks there before the professor said, "We can't keep this guy in kindergarten." They took me to the second grade, and before the year ended they sent me to third grade because I was so smart. I got promoted again and again, all the way to high school. Even though my siblings were all in school before me, I got an "A" before any one of them, so I graduated at the top of my high school.

My father was a police officer, a traffic director. After that, he left the police force and decided to go into business—diamonds. He got very successful, but then he wanted me to follow his footsteps, to forget about college and go to work in the diamond mine. I said, "What?! I'm getting good grades and you want me to go to the mines?"

He said, "Yup. Somebody has got to be there to take care of the family. You have to come, right now." So I went and joined him and started digging diamonds. My siblings were continuing school. That was a heartbreak for me because I really wanted to keep going to school. I was really focused on becoming a doctor, and I couldn't do that if I was shoveling and digging for diamonds.

I graduated in 1989, the same year the civil war in Liberia started. There were rebels starting to come, and I was in the village. I had a dream that the war was going to wipe out everybody. That morning I got up, took my bag, and just headed out for nowhere with a friend. My mother thought I was crazy. She said, "Where are you going?"

"I'm going to Guinea," I said.

She smiled and said, "You're crazy! You just got up from sleep."

I said, "I had a dream that the war that's coming is going to wipe out everybody. You think I'm kidding, Mom? I'm going, I'm leaving right now. I've got a friend, we've got a car, I'm leaving." So I got in the car and went to Guinea, and that was the end of 1989.

In 1990, the war started getting serious, but luckily I was already out of there. We had a lot of difficulties; I was in a border town by Liberia called Nzerekore. We didn't have jobs, and we didn't know anybody; I remember sleeping in the market. I get a little emotional thinking about that time. But the friend I was with was very hardworking. He knew a little bit about Guinea. We were able to work our way somehow. We even got a room, and we made a good living.

What actually blessed me was being an athlete. I played basketball, so I started playing for the town. I played basketball just for food. I became one of the best players. At that time, 1992, the war got really serious, refugees started fleeing, and I didn't know where my siblings were until the next year. Somebody told me that my sister was in Macenta, which was about eighty-five miles from where I was. I decided to go there and see my sister.

I lived with her and played basketball there again. I was happy. The town wanted me to play for them when they saw me practice—they have a national tournament from the capital city all over Guinea. So I played for Macenta. The team from the capital city saw me play, and that's when they recruited me.

When I got to the capital city, they started paying me money to play. While I was there, I was able to locate my siblings, and a lot of them moved to Guinea. By that time, my father was nowhere to be located. One of my father's friends was there, an international musician named Sekou Legrow Camara who played for the Bembeya Jazz International. I lived with him, and while I was living there, the diamond corporation opened. It was a branch of DeBeers, a diamond company based in London. At the time, my French was really good—all I spoke besides English was French and the local dialect called Soso. My father's friend saw me and said, "Listen, your dad and I were very good friends, but he's not here. There's a new company opening, and you speak English and French, so why don't you come and work for us? I'm doing this for your father." I took a position as the middleman between the buyer and the seller.

My mother is one of the role models in my life. Everybody in the family says that I act like my mom. She was very humble and loved to joke. She died when she was forty-two and never really got to see me working, doing something. I remember, when she got sick, I was in the village playing basketball for Macenta. I had to come back to the village to get her. She looked at me and didn't recognize me. She said "You look big! You coming from America or something?"

I said, "What do you mean? I come from the capital city of Conakry, not from America."

She said, "Well, I had a dream that you were in America."

I said, "Mom you're sick, let's go."

I put her in the car and took her to the city with me to have her healed. We drove with my elder sister, and I remember looking at my mom and the condition that she was in. She looked very badly off. The family couldn't even afford lotion at that time because of the war. They lost everything; there was no food, there was no money. Everybody was broke. Even me, I was struggling, but they were all looking at me. I had to share what little I had with every family member.

We stopped at a little village; I took my mom's hand, went down, and asked the people if I could get water. They said they had a well I could fetch water from. Her feet were so dirty, so dusty. I washed everything off, rubbed some lotion on her feet, and then brought her back to the car.

When we got to the city and I took my mother home, she said, "Go get me some water." I brought water. She said, "Put your feet in here." She was going to wash my feet too. I put my feet in there, and she washed them. When I went to the room to get a towel, my mother took the water she washed my feet with, and started to drink it!

I ran to her and said, "Why are you drinking that?"

She said, "I'm drinking this because you are a blessed child. I want to drink the water from your feet. You took me in your hands and went and washed my feet. It means a lot to me; you've given me everything in this world. When I drink that bowl where I washed your feet, I'm asking God, wherever he is in this world, to bless you. That's what I'm drinking this water for, so you are blessed everywhere you go. You are going to excel; you will always go far. Nothing is going to harm you."

Our people had strong beliefs, so when I left her to go get my visa to come to America, at first I didn't talk about it. I was trying to get my visa when I heard that my mom had died. But I had to go to America because it was time for me. I came back years later to see my mother's grave. I went to the village where she was buried. I saw the grave and prayed. After two years, my stepmother also died, so I left and came back again. I went back to Africa around 2013 to see my dad.

I was very successful, but I always had in the back of my mind, like every immigrant: *America, America*. It's a great place. When I was back home in Liberia, everything we saw of it on television was incredible. Growing up, we really didn't have that much difficulty in terms of food or clothing. My father was a little bit successful. But that doesn't cut it—people want to come to America because of curiosity and because they want to do something on their own. They hear about this great country and they want to come. When America is advertised to other nations, they don't show the ugly side.

In Africa, we didn't have all the rights that people have here in America. You couldn't say or do certain things. But America is a land of religious freedom, of freedom of expression. There are rules and regulations so that people feel safe; they want to live in that atmosphere. So my curiosity for America was always there, even though I was doing well working for De-Beers.

While I was working there I met a woman named Connie through my sister. She spoke French as well; she had been in the Peace Corps in Guinea before, and she loved it so much she moved back to Africa to live there. We started dating. She decided to go to America, and then she sent for me.

At first I didn't want to come: "I'm not going to leave my good job and my brothers and sisters here. I'm making good money, why should I go?" But then I thought, *All your friends are in America, America is the place to be, everybody is there. You know, why don't you go there?* I just started having these thoughts, and one day I decided, "*Okay, I'm going to go.*" I started searching for my visa to come to America.

It was 1995. I came in November, and it was wintertime. We had to take the train, and I'd never ridden the train before. I'd never even seen one outside of a magazine. Connie picked me up at JFK; I was very, very skinny. We came outside the door to get on the train—the first breeze that hit me, I felt like my ear was going to fall off if I touched it. Imagine, coming from Africa and the hot weather.

That was the first shock, and when I got on the train, I actually saw something that I didn't believe I was going to see. People were begging. I had just come from Africa, and a guy on a train was asking me to spare him a dime or nickel or something like that. I didn't know what dime was, what five cents or ten cents was. "Spare you a dime? What is this guy talking about?"

So my girlfriend Connie started laughing. "Dime, it means ten cents."

I said, "Really? This is how we're gonna start here? People begging on the streets?"

In Africa, people are a shame to their family if they are on the street. It would be difficult to get married if you had a family member who was on the street begging. Nowadays it's different, but back when I was growing up you didn't find any beggars because families tried to keep all their people off the street. There was a stigma; begging was against our norms.

Then here I was in America, where I thought everything was great, where you didn't have to beg because you were told that the moment you got to the airport people were running behind you looking to hire you! That's what people came and told us: "Oh yes, there are jobs; when you get to the airport there are jobs everywhere." That was my first shock, seeing the beggar on the train asking *me* for a dime

Then we got home, and all I wanted to eat was fried chicken! In Africa we used to see it in movies and TV: the fried chicken looked so good. When we arrived I was like, "Let's go get fried chicken first." I got some Popeye's, and I felt great.

Connie said, "Why don't we watch a movie?" We walked down the street to go to the Blockbuster, and I saw all these black guys living in Harlem on Lenox Avenue between 122nd and 125th. We tried to walk there and all these guys standing on the street said, "What the fuck are you doing with a white girl? Look at you, man, look at you, brother! Man, you make us all look bad man, you with a white girl." I was so confused.

Connie said, "Don't listen to them. They do that all the time." I thought that if this was how it was going to be, I was ready to go back to Africa. We didn't have crap like that. People not liking you for who you are, who you are hanging out with; what kind of country was this? I thought it was the greatest nation on earth. She said, "Well, you know, you got people on both sides who do things like that. White people do that same thing."

While I was in New York, Connie wanted to go to school, to get a master's degree. She got accepted to Tulane University, which she heard had a very good program. As she got ready to go, I decided to go back to school and get ready for Tulane.

We got to New Orleans—they called it N'awlins—and looked for a place to stay, but nobody would give us anywhere to rent because we were an interracial couple. Luckily, we found a man who was a former student at

Tulane University. He had graduated, and he and his wife had traveled all over the world and met many international students. He was able to rent us a place, and he told us why we were having the difficulties that we were. He said that since we were an interracial couple, it was going to be hard to find a place to rent.

I got into Tulane ready to do business, and my academic advisor said, "Why do all the Africans want to do either business or political science?" I said that I didn't know—I actually wanted to be a doctor. She said, "Why don't you do that? You're an athlete, and I know that Africa needs physical therapy." I think my advisor was in Africa for a long time when people had broken legs—lots of people ended up being crippled, and there was no on-site physical therapy or orthopedic surgeons. A lot of people were handicapped when they could have been taken good care of elsewhere. So she said, "Why don't you become one of those?"

I decided to give physiology a try. I thought it was almost like being a doctor. I wanted to help people get in shape if they had a bad knee problem or something. And besides that, it was a little more challenging for me.

When we left New Orleans, I started working at New York Sports Club in New Jersey. I was the training manager. Connie, now my wife, went to work in New York. At that time, we had just had a daughter, and I decided that the best place to bring up a child would be in the Midwest—Connie was from Wisconsin and had lived in Winona, MN, so we decided to come here. Besides that, I had applied for resettlement for my siblings to come to the United States, and one of the states that accepted them was Minnesota through Lutheran Social Services. It was a good match.

They were supposed to come on September 17, 2001, but 9/11 stopped everything. I was in New Jersey at the time. The government put a stop to refugees coming from countries that didn't have anything to do with terrorism. Africa was part of that—all those refugees from all over the world were stopped from coming. It took another two or three years for my siblings to arrive.

I decided to pursue the reasons why my family had been stopped for moving here. Norm Coleman had just been elected. I decided to walk into his office on University Avenue. The first day he was in office I walked in, and Jones, a case worker, was there. I explained the situation to her and she said, "Whoa! That's a great story, but as you can see, we're just setting the table, we haven't even set everything up. I'm going to follow your story because there's no reason why your brothers and sisters should not be here. Especially since they didn't have anything to do with the terrorist act. And we have refugees coming from other parts of the world, so why are they stopping your siblings from coming?" She followed the story, and in around two or three weeks, my siblings were here in the United States.

Norm Coleman worked very hard to make sure that they got here. It was actually on the news a few times; we had a few interviews, talking about how difficult it was. The difficulties we had related to the stigma that you have as an immigrant or a refugee when you come to America. People feel that if you are an immigrant, you are not educated. They feel that you're starving. They feel that you're a criminal. You have all of these stereotypes toward you, and that can be very, very difficult.

Back home, when we see foreigners coming, we welcome them! We get happy, we want to know them! But for me it was the opposite in America. Everywhere that you go, people look at you like you're different. You have an accent. And at some point you get embarrassed to even get into the crowd because they always say your name wrong. I have to say my name maybe two or three times before somebody can pronounce it. How difficult is "Amara"? Then you wonder if they are doing it intentionally as an insult, if they just want to make a mockery out of you. So you put all of these thoughts into your head. You feel that maybe you don't fit into this society.

When I came to Minneapolis, I started working with Lifetime Fitness downtown. While I was there, I met a friend of mine, also from Liberia. He had his own business maybe five or six miles down the road, where he was doing personal training. I started working with him part time while I was at Lifetime, and eventually I decided to completely move there and work with him, where I was able to get a share of the business. Unfortunately, he decided that we were going to move his gym's location. I said that we couldn't move the gym because we were doing so well. But he moved anyway, and we lost all our customers.

A friend of mine, who was also working with us as a personal trainer, opened another gym. He said, "Hey, listen, we can work together and you don't have to open another facility. You can use this; you can bring all your customers here and help pay the rent. You have your own business within this business." So we moved there. Ever since then, for about ten years now, I've been doing my own business. That was the best move I ever made. I'm able to schedule my own time and go on vacation if I want to. The downside is that if I don't work, I don't get paid, so I have to consistently keep working.

People perceive immigrants as incapable, which isn't true. So many immigrants that I know, in Brooklyn Park and the Twin Cities, have businesses that hire Americans to work for them and pay their taxes every time. I don't even get money back. I pay taxes every time. How can we be failing to contribute to the country when I have two American-born employees?

I'm so proud because under my own umbrella, those employees were able to start their own personal training businesses. I trained them to become successful business people. We'll get together and even share ideas. Besides doing that, I've done a lot of things for the community. Not only mine, not only the African community, but in the broader American community, everybody working together as a team.

I have the entrepreneurial mindset because my father was a businessman when he left the police. I always admired him when he got dressed up to go to work, and I wanted to be something like that. My entire family were business people; they liked to work for themselves. So that was already in me, especially being a Mandinka; we are a tribe of business people.

One of my projects is called the Dandies Project. Its first mission was to deal with men of color within the community who didn't know each other, who were not connected. It brought them together to do a photographic exhibit and book and to serve as role models for kids, to teach kids how to dress properly. The way you present yourself is how people perceive you. That was the whole mission, for the black community to have some leaders, because I saw that Martin Luther King, Jr. and my dad, when they dressed up, spoke with their clothes before they even opened their mouths. I've led the project for the last two years. Its mission has now changed so that instead of men of color, everybody is involved. We've been very successful—you can't believe how many people came to embrace the project and all want to be part of it.

We do the project every year. We look for the photographer who's going to do the photo shoot. We dress these guys up. We solicit clothes from boutiques as sponsors, or we bring our own clothes. We do the photo shoot. The proceeds from the books go to a nonprofit organization that is really struggling. One of these nonprofits was Lovely's Sewing and Arts Collective which teaches kids how to sew. We watch people like that and give them the proceeds every year.

I help the economy of this country; I am not just sitting there and doing nothing. I love this country. It has given me the opportunity to see things differently and to live the way I want to live, and I appreciate that. But people should appreciate immigrants, who we are as people. Every nation has bad people and good people. There are bad Americans, and there are bad immigrants. But you can't put everybody in the same box and just lock them up. That's totally wrong.

Don't have a wavering mind. Stop considering everything—focus. Often people have all these different things they are jumping between—going from wanting to be a movie star to wanting to be a doctor—and not focusing on one thing. Not focusing will put fears in you and that is going to limit your abilities. You have to be patient, be consistent, and don't listen to anybody who says you can't. Follow your dream. That is how I became successful.

I'm still not where I want to be, and trust me, I have people telling me, "Hey, Amara, this isn't working for you, why don't you try something else?" But they don't know where I started; I'm not there anymore. I'm growing, and I'm going to be what I want to be. You have to be very consistent and believe in yourself. Belief is one of the key things. Follow your dream and stop listening to people putting fears in you.

My dad always told me, "You haven't lived a life, Amara, if you haven't impacted someone else's life." Doing business, I feel like I have the opportunity to make an impact on my family's life. I get tired of this paycheck-to-paycheck. I want to be who I am now, and everybody in my family looks at me like I am somebody who brings the bread, whether they live here or in Africa. Fighting to have my own business might help in the long run.

I am happy where I am now. I got divorced, maybe ten years ago, but we have two lovely kids. My daughter, Manya, is sixteen. My son, Abraham, is thirteen. I really enjoy my time with them. They're sweet, smart kids. They go to Catholic school in Winona, where they live with their mom.

I got remarried to the woman I love. Her name is Tenin Conde. What I like about her is that we both speak the same language, and we're both Muslim. That has changed my life in so many different ways. I always wanted to marry someone from my tribe, but I didn't have the opportunity to do that before. Now that I'm married to Tenin, I see a whole different lifestyle for me—going back to my country, my roots, and doing some of the things that I used to do back there. I miss all those things, because I couldn't do them with my ex. I'm getting back into my community, which I was away from for a while; I really love that. Sometimes I'll take little trips with her—we'll go to the movies, or just sit in the car and drive around the city, just to see different things. I really enjoy these things.

I'm president of the Dandies Project, which I really enjoy, and am also former president of operations for the Liberian Project in the United States. I presently serve as the administrator for the Musji Islamic Community Center. I really enjoy my time being an entrepreneur, and helping my community move forward. That is my lifestyle.

MEDIA LINKS

greencardvoices.org/speakers/amara-kamara

Sylhet,
Bangladesh

Ruhel Islam

From: Sylhet, Bangladesh
Current City: Minneapolis, MN

Current Business:
Gandhi Mahal Restaurant
gandhimahal.com

> "YOU HAVE TO WORK HARD FOR THAT DREAM AND HAVE GOOD INTENTIONS. ONLY THEN CAN SUCH A DREAM BECOME REALITY, BUT YOU ALSO HAVE TO GIVE IT BACK TO YOUR COMMUNITY. THE MORE YOU GIVE BACK, THE MORE IT COMES BACK TO YOU!"

The country I was born and raised in has a population half that of the United States that is condensed into an area the size of the state of Iowa. For the inquisitive mind, the country I'm referring to is Bangladesh. I was raised in a big family, one of seven children—two boys and five girls. I, the fourth child, am the younger of the boys. My father was a businessman who primarily focused on agriculture, while my mother was a housewife (and, more importantly, a great mother). My uncle was one of the longest-serving finance ministers in the nation's history and the architect of the Bangladesh economy. Furthermore, he was a notable member of the Bangladesh judiciary system, serving as the Justice of Bangladesh.

During my childhood, I spent most of my time in the rural area of the country. As a little boy, I was highly proactive in the community; I was planting trees, fishing, collecting donations, and participating in relief work for floods and other natural disasters, as well as just running around and participating in sports. In my first business venture as a child, I started with two chickens and eventually ended up with two thousand.

My sister got married to an American businessman, and my uncle arranged a visa for me to accompany her to the United States. This was most definitely a life-changing experience, one that words cannot describe. There was, of course, another reason I had to leave my family behind: politics. The nation was deteriorating due to power struggles between major political parties. This is a natural occurrence in Bangladesh. Every term one party comes into power while everyone else from the opposition party goes on a strike— sometimes you are caught on the wrong side, which tends to invite trouble. As I was one of the grassroots level organizers for my uncle's constituency, I had to leave. My father said, "Don't come back!"

On my way to America, I stopped over in London, where I stayed for a few days with family and friends whom I hadn't seen for years. I arrived in New York City on April 9, 1996; it was the last day of snow. That was very shocking to me, but I felt joy and happiness as I watched the snow fall, like I was experiencing an act of divinity. It looked heavenly. I felt a feeling of serenity, peace, and joy, like nothing I had ever felt.

The experience of being in a different land was a complete cultural shock for me. I had to sacrifice many things that I held dear to me. As my father had told me not to return, I never got to see him again. A couple of years after we parted, he passed away; my mother joined him soon after. I was separated from family, friends, and my livelihood.

In the beginning, the little things were good. The ever-changing weather threw some rough curves—the snow was much different from what I had anticipated. Life in New York seemed good since my sister was nearby, but eventually it became tough, or at least felt that way for me. Things seemed to ease up eventually once I got a job in a restaurant.

My brother came to the US in 1994, moved to Minneapolis in 1998 to start a business, and stayed there. I first visited Minneapolis in 2000 and later decided to settle in 2005. This city became my home and my life. It's a lot different from New York—Minneapolis, to me, is the best city in the entire world. Even as a complete stranger, I found everyone very welcoming. Here people understand cross-cultural dialogue. We have a lot of culturally diverse people living in the area, especially around the place I live right now. Many of the activities I did in my youthful years in Bangladesh, I can do here: fishing, exploring nature, growing my own herbs and food. When I took my oath of citizenship, the judge said, "We don't want you to forget your culture; we want you to bring your culture." That inspired me a lot, and becoming a US citizen was one of my biggest dreams come true.

Due to the chances and opportunities that were granted to me, in 2008 I started one of the most sustainable aquaponic restaurants in the country. This establishment, which I worked tirelessly to build, provides healthy food and mostly locally-sourced produce. In the local community, I have grown my own vegetables from the beginning and participated in community gardens. The business has patronized local food sources and gotten involved with different civic groups by stirring up discussions on important issues such as food security. I'm also currently part of the local food organization and serve as the president of the local business council.

As a child, agriculture was an important factor in my life, and even to this day, I continuously labor for and advocate the importance of agriculture in our contemporary society. It's possible to promote such important issues because in Minneapolis, people come together to help you out with anything you need in order to create a more just and meaningful society. Currently, we source and stockpile over ten thousand pounds of vegetables from local gardens and markets. Another initiative we have undertaken is giving ex-offenders from a halfway house, Volunteers of America (VOA), a second chance by providing them jobs so they can start a fresh new beginning with references. We also provide support for the youth group at Restorative Justice and fund a scholarship program dedicated to the memory of my uncle.

We have received the Community Responsibility Award as an acknowledgment of our sustainability efforts to make the world a better place; we have also received recognition from the media, grassroots-level activists, and leaders of various communities who encouraged us to be more dedicated and to further our sustainability efforts and work. Since I'm more of an action guy, I suggested making the community room in our restaurant. The community room is a spot where anyone can go; it's a gathering place for meaningful conversations about the exchange and implementation of ideas and knowledge. We've hosted many legislative updates for high officials, and the room has been declared a Peace Site for the World Citizens. The community room is one of many ways that the restaurant gives back to the community, besides contributing a part of our proceeds. I am a strong proponent of giving back to the community. I believe that working together can bring real peace to the world and is the only way to achieve what your heart desires.

When I started my restaurant business, we named it after Gandhi. We thought it was the right time to name it after such a notable and monumental figure, one who played an important role in history and advocated a simple concept: bringing people together and promoting cross-cultural dialogue. We wanted to remind everyone of Gandhi's struggle for a better world, a world without violence. When you are hungry, you're angry. Only food can bring us together. As Gandhi once famously stated, "God comes to the hungry in the form of food." Come to the table! Eat vegetarian, nonvegetarian, halal, or kosher; drink wine or beer; and start a conversation so we can bring real peace to the world. We indulge ourselves with nourishment, not only for the satisfaction of our stomach but also for our souls. The philosophy is that we all know each other, no strangers—this is how we succeed in the community.

Our motto is "Dedicated to bringing peace by pleasing your palate."

During my initial business years, I faced various challenges and spoke out, not only to talk about problems that existed but also to present solutions that might remedy these problems. I have spoken in various forums, such as public council hearings at the city and state level. Furthermore, I participated in a roundtable discussion at the White House Business Council. I, along with forty-five other small business owners from Minneapolis, discussed the importance of small businesses and how they can play a more pivotal role in the overall US economy. I was given the opportunity to talk with the committee about food security, how my business started, and what kind of support was needed from the White House. The next day, I was fortunate enough to meet the British prime minister and to see the Obamas. I also had an opportunity to meet a half-Bangladeshi lady who was an assistant cabinet secretary to the President of the United States. Everywhere you go you will find a Bangla-speaking person. This world is very small; it's a global village. You can find everything.

I'm very happy here now. I have a family: a beautiful wife and three beautiful daughters. I have my own business, my friends, and of course my extended family. My brother and cousins also reside here in Minneapolis. Every day I meet a lot of amazing individuals, through either business, specific groups, organizations, or the community. They are all wonderful people.

Since I am awake, the American dream is not a dream anymore; it's a reality. There was no real freedom in Bangladesh, but here in America, we have so much freedom and opportunity; we can speak our minds and work hard to achieve our desires. We as Bengalis do not have a big community here in Minneapolis, but I think the entire neighborhood is my community, and this is how I approach my life and work. It's not easy to do business coming from another country, but this is a wonderful nation that gives you an opportunity, especially here in Minneapolis, to achieve your dreams and goals. You have to have a dream and you have to believe in your dream, but most importantly, you have to work hard for that dream and have good intentions. Only then can such a dream become reality, but you also have to give it back to your community. The more you give back, the more it comes back to you!

MEDIA LINKS

greencardvoices.org/speakers/ruhel-islam

Torreon,
Mexico

Manila,
Philippines

they did arts and crafts on Friday afternoon, but otherwise there were no studio spaces or gallery spaces that were accessible. I feel like our biggest contribution to where we immigrated to and where we graduated from, which is the East Side, is putting a space like Indigenous Roots Cultural Arts Center in our community.

MEDIA LINKS

greencardvoices.org/speakers/mary-anne-sergio-quiroz

Calabria, Italy

Caterina Cerano

From: Calabria, Italy
Current City: Minneapolis, MN

Current Business:

Alterations by Caterina

> "I WAS VERY GOOD AT WHAT I DID. I SET AN EXAMPLE FOR PEOPLE; THEY KNEW MY WORK TOOK ALL MY HEART. I TREATED CUSTOMERS HOW I WOULD WANT TO BE TREATED."

I was born in Calabria, Italy. At the time, it was a very small little town. I am the oldest of eight children, and it was hard for me; I went to school until fifth grade, at which point I began doing chores and washing clothes by hand. I took care of my siblings so they could go to school, and then I stayed home to clean and cook. My mother was working a little; my father was working all the time. We didn't even have water inside the house.

In 1970, my great-aunt came from America to Italy to meet my grandmother and her brother for the first time; she had left Italy when they were little children. She saw that my father had a big family that was living one day at a time and doing the best they could, so she went back to America and she tried to sponsor me; that way my grandma could come to America and meet her brother and other sister, who had been born there. She completed the paperwork, and my dad, my grandma, and I went to the American consulate in Naples. The American counselor told my grandma that I could not go to America because I was underage—only sixteen.

My grandma said, "Well, if she cannot come, I'm not going either."

He changed his mind. "Okay, I'll let her go with you." My grandma ended up staying for three months, and I stayed longer.

Before coming to the United States, my mom and my dad went to Milano to say goodbye to another son my grandmother had over there. After that, I took the plane from Malpensa. I can still see my mom waving a white handkerchief and crying her lungs out as the airplane left the airport.

When we came to the United States, I think they must have messed up the communication between the agency in Italy and my family here in America—when we landed in Chicago, there was nobody there. A very kind black person—I had never met anyone black before—said, "We can take you to the hotel." But we didn't want to go to the hotel because we didn't speak English, so we stayed at the airport. They gave us sandwiches, and we ate. We tried to call my uncle and my aunt Catherine, who had sponsored me, but they didn't answer their phone, so we had to spend the night at the airport. I remember that we were very scared. The next day, they found out where we were and got us in a hurry.

When we got here, we stayed with my aunt Carolina in Illinois while Catherine was on vacation. I did not like the bread here; it was like cotton balls! I didn't like any of their food, or their salad. Carolina was very kind and used to go to the bakery shop to buy Vienna bread. It was crispier. Every morning I would get sick and throw up, and my aunt thought, "Oh my God, maybe she came to America to have a baby!" So she took me to the doctor, and he said to her, "She's not pregnant, she just has a nervous stomach!" It's the same as if you were to go to Italy, to a different world; you would have thrown up too. My aunt was relieved.

Later, Aunt Catherine found me a job because I was the only one with a visa. I used to take the bus from her apartment to South Robert Street. In the winter, I would walk, crying—it was too cold, and all I could do was cut the edge of draperies because I didn't know how to speak English.

I still remember, though, that there were so many great people. There was this old lady who looked in a dictionary to translate for me. My great-aunt sent me to the International Institute twice a week. When my English was good enough, the director of the institute told me that I was ready to learn a skill. She sent me to the Technical Vocational Institute, which is now St. Paul College. She only paid ten dollars for the yearbook, and everything else was free. My skill was apparel arts, learning about sewing and machinery.

My first job was at Foreman & Clark. At the time, I was not yet a resident, so they paid me cash until my paperwork was done. As soon as the paperwork was finished and I got my green card, the job was official. I had a bit of a hard time with the supervisor of the alterations shop. She was from Yugoslavia, and while she meant well, she was too controlling. She used to say when I would come to work a little tired, "What did you do last night?" When I would tell her, "That's none of your business!" she would get mad.

This continued until a friend who lived in my building died. I wanted to go to her funeral, but my supervisor would not let me. She said to me, "If you go to the funeral, don't come back to work." I said, "That's fine! I'm not coming back to work." So the manager, George Brasheer, who called me

Kathy, said, "You go to your friend's funeral and come back whenever you want, today or tomorrow." And it was okay. The supervisor was very angry because the manager understood the way I felt about my friend. But now we are very good friends.

I worked there for a long time. I was very good at what I did. I set an example for people; they knew my work took all my heart. I treated customers how I would want to be treated. But toward the end, managers started to treat me very poorly. The last one was at Men's Wearhouse—this young manager used to tell me to watch the clock when I went into the fitting room with people. I said, "No, I'm not going to rush to fit the customer!" I was a fast worker. I didn't need him to stand behind my back. One day he wrote me a note telling me to time myself—and I took the note and threw it in the garbage with my face red as fire. I decided to quit before I had a stroke.

After that job, I got another one, and so on. I believe it was 2006 when someone at my job said that, if I wanted to have a business of my own, he had a tiny room I could rent. So I did that for a while. Unfortunately, he was also in control, telling me when I could or couldn't go on a vacation. I always provided him with another person so he would not be stranded by himself to do alterations. After a while, I got tired of that. During my breaks I would go down to St. Peter's Street and call my kids. My daughter was so little, and I realized this was too much, too much—the work was so lousy. I decided to go on my own.

My son helped me to finish the room that was my store. As a single mother, I had always feared for my children's futures should I strike out on my own, but a friend of mine told me, "Caterina, you should open your own shop." I thought this was like God giving me a kind of sign: You can do better than this!

Now I work for myself, making beautiful dresses. I have a person help me two or three times a week. Of course there have been hardships; I'm still nervous about making it. Whatever I need to do always costs money. I have a nice spot now, but it's always a challenge to come up with a thousand dollars a month to pay the rent. I used to be in the Lowry Building, and the landlords always sympathized with me and kept the rent as low as they could. Now I have a different landlord, but they are also very nice.

I get nervous when it slows down, but I have repeat customers who are always happy to come over and give me compliments. I've made a lot of friends because of this; they enjoy staying to chat and have coffee sometimes.

I like being here—I have a little kitchen, I make coffee whenever I want, and I have pictures on the wall. It's just like my second home. I could not ask for better.

When you need to bend, you bend. When you need to help somebody and do things a little cheaper, it's okay. Many times for the last couple of years I've been making prom dresses for a program, some of them for free, others with a discount. Whenever you do something for another, God will reward you. Sometimes I am scared, but on the other hand, I feel like God is watching. He has never let me down.

I have two beautiful children, now adults, and a very nice-looking grandson. My children help me a lot. I'm happy. I live with my daughter in a nice home; she keeps an eye on me. I like to stay home too, to enjoy my house. I am still independent, though—I travel to see my Italian friends.

I love and respect America. I never regret coming here, even though I left my whole family back in Italy. Back in 1986, we had an American military base where we lived. My heart leaped when I saw American soldiers! Seeing them, seeing the American flag, I would I feel at home. I feel more at home here than in Italy.

MEDIA LINKS

greencardvoices.org/speakers/caterina-cerano

Biên Hòa,
Vietnam

MEDIA LINKS

greencardvoices.org/speakers/trung-pham

Managua,
Nicaragua

Marcia Malzahn

From: Managua, Nicaragua

Current City: Maple Grove, MN

Current Business:

Malzahn Strategic

malzahnstrategic.com

> "SOMETIMES WE ONLY FOCUS ON THE FINANCIAL SIDE OF THINGS, AND WE FORGET THE EMOTIONAL PART OF STARTING A BUSINESS."

My life in Nicaragua was happy and peaceful. I was the second of six children. My dad was an attorney and a composer, and my mom—a home-maker at first—later became an entrepreneur. Our life was very good until I was thirteen years old. During those thirteen years, I experienced four major events that left a mark on my life.

The first event was the earthquake in 1972—it happened December 23, the night before Christmas Eve. I was only six years old and I still remember it like it was yesterday. It was a terrifying experience. About ten thousand people died in Managua, and I could have been one of them. After the first two intense tremors, I moved to my parents' bedroom and slept with them. During the earthquake, their two beds, which had been pushed together, became separated; I fell in between them. My parents couldn't find me. I remember hearing my mom's voice in the distance, somewhere in the dark. She finally found my foot and carried me out of the room and into the backyard, where we all met.

Because of the extensive damage to our home, my parents had to build a new house away from the earthquake's epicenter. We moved to another city, Leon, until the new house was built. The infrastructure of the new house was built for earthquakes, but not necessarily for the wars which happened several years later.

The second event to leave a mark on me occurred when I was eleven years old. My parents sent me to San Francisco as an exchange student to learn English. Although this was a good experience for me, it was also somewhat traumatic to be separated from my family for three months, including Christmas, at such a young age.

The third event happened during 1978–79, when the revolution against the decades-long Somoza dictatorship started in Nicaragua. At that time, I had the opportunity to come to the United States once again as an exchange student, and I chose the same family who had hosted me before. This time, the experience was much more enjoyable, but when I returned in February 1979 things were worse in Nicaragua. The Sandinistas were advancing, about to overthrow the government. I was thirteen years old, and my parents learned that the Sandinistas were sending children as young as fourteen years old into battle.

This was one of many reasons for us to leave. The political situation in Nicaragua was going from a dictatorship to a communist regime. That was going to change everything. The religious situation was also a key decision factor; we were a Christian family and the rising communist regime was atheist. Economically speaking, the country was in chaos. The grocery stores had no food to buy, and the electricity and water kept being cut off during the last few months of our stay. We had to leave.

The only country we could flee to at that time was the Dominican Republic. My dad's sister had married a Dominican, and they offered up their home for my family to move into. It was June 24, 1979, two weeks before the Sandinista revolution overthrew the Somoza dictatorship. My father was fifty years old at the time, my mom thirty-five. I was thirteen, and my siblings were one-and-a-half, two-and-a-half, ten, eleven, and fourteen.

There were no more commercial airlines coming to the country anymore. My dad heard there was a Red Cross cargo plane coming to Nicaragua to take out the people from El Salvador, so we left our home, even the dog, with the maids. We arrived at the airport at six in the morning and approached the pilot to see if we could get on the plane.

The pilot told my dad, "No, there is no room for you and your family. This plane is full and it's only for people from El Salvador."

My dad said nothing, but while the pilot was busy putting people in the plane, my dad started loading the twenty-six pieces of luggage that we brought with us. All of a sudden, the pilot realizes there was a pile of suitcases in the plane with no owners.

The pilot asked, "Whose luggage is all this?"

My dad replied, "It's mine and my family's."

The pilot said "But I already told you there is no room for your family."

And then my dad said, "I'll make you a deal. I'll exchange suitcases for each one of my kids and my wife. I'll stay behind." And the pilot agreed. My mom and the two little ones got in, then my older sister and my other brother.

Then, my eleven-year-old sister, the quiet one of our family, said, "Our dad shouldn't stay behind alone. I'll stay with him." I saw a little tear coming out of her left eye and said, "No, that's not right. I'm older than you. I'll stay with our dad." And she got on the plane.

At that time, I remember standing to my dad's left and thinking to myself, "This was a bad idea!" I felt the worst feeling of abandonment, a feeling I'll never forget. You know when you get lost and you get that horrible feeling in your gut and you just want to cry? That's how I felt. But then, all of the sudden like in a movie, my dad traded more suitcases and I was on the plane. He stood on the runway with twenty-five suitcases—mine made it on the plane. And we took off. I watched my father get smaller and smaller in the distance. We didn't know if we would ever see him again.

But God performed a miracle for our family. There was a single passenger plane en route from Argentina to Costa Rica that needed to refuel in Nicaragua. They had a single seat open. My dad got on the plane and asked the Red Cross people at the airport to send all our luggage to El Salvador. We reunited there, and a couple of days later we all flew to the Dominican Republic, where they took us in as refugees of war.

My aunt converted her office into a bedroom for my parents and put the baby's crib there. The the rest of us five kids lived in the one-car garage, but we were not sad and did not complain. My cousin found a picture of us from that time; in it, we are all smiling. We were so happy to be alive and free!

Two months later we moved to a two-bedroom, fourth-floor apartment, and my family survived yet another disaster. Hurricane David hit the island at 175 mph and devastated it. I was still only thirteen! But not one window broke in our apartment. We spent the next three months with no water or electricity. My family was safe again, happy to be alive.

We lived in the Dominican Republic for almost seven years. My dad had left his music career a while before and decided to pursue law. However, the Dominican Republic had a different code of law, so he switched to selling life insurance. My mom, who had been a homemaker, became an entrepreneur. She started baking bread; she would send my two younger brothers and sister to the grocery store to sell loaves at the door because she didn't have permission to sell them inside. She started sewing uniforms for schools, and then started a small jewelry business selling in consignment. Two things happened through the jewelry business. I got my first job, volunteering to be my mother's bookkeeper. Then she became a certified jeweler and obtained her jeweler's certification in Miami, Florida.

We had always known that we were going to come to the United States, but we hadn't known when or how long the preparation to get here was going to take. As a next step, our parents opened an official branch of the business in Miami, Florida. That way, we could obtain legal visas for both my parents and the two oldest kids, my sister and me. When we arrived, she was twenty and I was nineteen.

At a Christian event in the Dominican Republic, my parents had met some people who lived in the Twin Cities, and they fell in love with us. They told my parents, "We will help you come to the United States. We will open our homes. You guys just finish the legal part." My parents came here for the first time to scope it out in January 1985—the coldest time of the year! They decided that the people were so nice that the weather didn't matter to them.

When I came here with my older sister later in 1985, it was summer, so of course we loved it and went back saying that people were awesome. We then started planning the move for the entire family. My brother, who was fourteen, came in August to start school, staying with a family in Minneapolis. My younger sister came second, staying with a family in St. Paul and also enrolled in school. My turn came the following January, and I stayed in St. Paul. My older sister came in April and stayed with another family in Minneapolis. Lastly, my parents came in June with the two younger ones, and we all reunited after almost a year. We started renting a house in Edina. We were so happy to be together again.

In 1979, when I left Nicaragua at thirteen, we had to leave everything behind, even our Barbies, all our toys, our dog—everything we had. My parents had owned five homes, including a beach house. Those memories of going to the beach every weekend are some of the best that I have. Sometimes I think that when we left our life behind, my parents left part of their identity behind as well. That part was very, very hard to recover, if that was even possible, and especially in a different country. Even in the Dominican Republic, which is a Latin American country that speaks Spanish, they have a different culture. They have a different history. All my parents' friends were gone. Their relatives were gone, dispersed to different countries, so they left a lot behind.

I left all my friends in Nicaragua, and there was no email or cell phones in 1986 to stay connected. I never saw some of those friends again. In the Dominican Republic, I left behind all my best friends from my teenage years. My most valuable possession in both countries was the friends I left. That's why I now feel that I'm so attached to people. To me, friendships are like a treasure. They're like gold.

That's why I am also so attached to this country. This is my land now, my home, and I don't want to leave ever again—even Minnesota, despite the horribly cold weather.

Life here was different in every way. The people were awesome, welcoming, and loving, but it was a different culture. I am personally very expressive, very into hugging and touching—here, especially in the business world, a lot of people are much less expressive than me. "Don't touch anybody!" is what you hear. People have bubbles. And I say, "I have no bubble." Adjusting to this could be hard.

I thought I spoke English, but when I came here, I was confused not only by slang (which still confuses me), but also differing words like "pop" and "soda." I didn't know which was right. I also didn't know business English, so I had to learn it very quickly. I had very little work experience. I came here when I was nineteen and had only been a secretary at my university in the Dominican Republic and bookkeeper to my mom's small jewelry business.

Lastly, education was a challenge I faced. One of my strengths from the StrengthsFinder Assessment is "Learner." For me, not being able to go to school was a huge sacrifice. I couldn't finish the degree I had started in Dominican Republic for a long, long time. My mission was to find a job so I wouldn't be a burden to this country or to anyone else. I stayed with the family who hosted me until my parents arrived in June that year. Little did I know that it was going to take me twenty-seven years to finish my college degree. That is a whole story in itself.

My job as a bookkeeper helped me find a job as a teller at a bank because I could count money. Then I got a job as a secretary because of my work for the university's president. Those two jobs were the beginning of my twenty-three-year banking career. Throughout my career, I experienced many challenges, but they were mostly those of a woman rising to the executive ranks in banking, rather than a result of my being a first-generation immigrant or Latina.

I never wanted to be an entrepreneur. Having observed my parents, who were both entrepreneurs, I saw how much income could fluctuate and never wanted to experience that. I am a planner, and I like to plan on a set income—even if it's small. However, I did inherit an entrepreneurial spirit from my parents. After thirty-two years of work experience (twenty-three years in banking and five years in nonprofits), I had accumulated a lot of valuable business experience—especially after the last ten years overseeing all areas of operations for a bank I helped start. I decided to pursue my dreams instead of that career. I saw an amazing opportunity to pursue the three things that I love the most: bank consulting, speaking, and writing. I wanted to help community banks become operationally stronger, and I wanted to inspire people to be the best they can be through my speaking and writing.

I am what they call a "solopreneur," meaning I don't intend to build a big business. I need to stay on my own and have the flexibility to pursue my dreams and my mission in life, which is to help working people be successful in every area of their lives.

I have been an entrepreneur for almost four years now, and I have to admit, as I'm sure most entrepreneurs would agree, it has been challenging in many ways. Making the jump from a full-time bank executive to being on my own, with no employees, no support, and no paycheck, was a challenge. But being the planner I am, I prepared my exit for an entire year before I left my job. My first goal was to train all my direct reports. I delegated all the critical functions that needed to be done for the bank to continue being successful. The next goal was to promote all my employees to the highest level I could. That was my gift to each one as a thank-you for their loyalty and hard work. Then I planned the financial part. I needed a cushion to replace my contribution to the household income. I sold my ownership of the bank to have that cushion.

My large network of friends and professionals, along with the marketing strategies I put into place, helped me to start the bank consulting business Malzahn Strategic. The business of public speaking, on the other hand, was all new to me. Even though I had been speaking for over fifteen years (mostly pro bono), going "from free to fee" is the biggest challenge when you decide to pursue speaking as a profession.

Being an immigrant as an entrepreneur has not made any difference in my case, either with hardships or with special opportunities—other than people making fun of my accent, which is a great icebreaker in conversations.

All my bank clients are not immigrants, and I "grew up" in my banking career and rose to the executive ranks working with older white males. The challenge, for the most part, has been usually being the only female executive in the senior leadership team and in the boardroom. I'm sure most women in the financial services industry can relate with me on this.

As a professional speaker, however, I find that being an immigrant gives me an amazing opportunity to share my story—both the larger story of being an immigrant entrepreneur in America and my own life story. People find these stories fascinating, and I love sharing them because I can use them to inspire people all over the world. My mission when I speak is to inspire and educate my audience. I do this whether I'm teaching a bank webinar or doing the keynote at a business women's leadership conference.

The biggest lesson I've learned is that you must have a plan—for everything—and then be flexible enough to deal with changes along the way. Sometimes we only focus on the financial side of things and we forget the emotional part of starting a business. I wrote an article (published on LinkedIn) called "Leading through Entrepreneur Depression" when I came across this concept and realized I had gone through entrepreneur depression. I don't regularly suffer from depression, but I think I experienced it for a while during my first year as an entrepreneur, when I was alone. I felt lonely and anxious about everything regarding the business. I missed being an executive and making daily decisions that would impact an entire organization. I missed developing my employees. I missed being part of a team. It took two years to get used to working on my own and know that it was all okay. Now I look forward to working from home all day on client projects, my next presentation, an article, or my next book. I have made the choice to do this for the rest of my life. I have found my calling, and pursuing your calling is the most fulfilling thing you can do. I encourage you to find your calling and pursue it too.

My life in the United States has been a blessing. I love the people and I love America. This is my country and my home now. I am so grateful to God for sending me to this country full of opportunities, and that's why, in July 1996, I took the oath to become an American citizen. My life now that my kids are grown is still full, but it's different. This year marks my thirtieth wedding anniversary with my beloved Minnesotan husband, Tim. My work consists of consulting with small financial institutions on strategic planning, enterprise risk management, and talent management. I speak to three audiences: banking, women business leaders, and faith-based audiences. I present inspirational keynotes at banking and women's leadership conferences, banking seminars, webinars with banking associations, and small women's groups at churches and ministries. I write consistently on Saturdays, working on either one of the four books I'm writing or business and leadership articles.

I also love to volunteer my time and talents to serve on the boards of nonprofit organizations. I have done so for the past twenty-five years. I'm currently on the Board of InFaith Community Foundation and Shine in the World Ministries. I also volunteer to go on mission trips abroad. In 2016, I went to Kigali, Rwanda. In 2018, I went to Nicaragua to do a short mission trip with my parents, who founded a nonprofit to help the poor. Later in 2018, I'll be going to the Dominican Republic on a trip with Hope International. I want to repay them for the generosity and kindness they bestowed upon me when I was a refugee in their beautiful country.

I'm proud that I have never been a burden to this country. I didn't come here with any sense of being entitled to help from any individual or the government. Instead, I work, I pay my taxes, and I contribute to society. I love people; I love mentoring the younger generation through nonprofits such as Big Brothers Big Sisters and Way to Grow. I'm big on education because I think it's one of the keys to success in America and every other country in the world. I also serve the poor with other organizations such as Opportunity International, which took me back to Nicaragua in December of 2012.

I want to help nonprofit organizations that help the poor to become self-sustainable, obtain education, gain work experience, and form connections. Those are some of the things I do. I have also written three books. I wrote Devotions for Working Women: A Daily Inspiration to Live a Successful and Balanced Life (2006) to help working women who are trying their best to be successful in their careers and strive to be balanced at home. I then wrote The Fire Within: Connect Your Gifts with Your Calling (2015) to encourage people to discover their talents and connect them with their mission in life. I wrote my third book, The Friendship Book: Because You Matter to Me, which is meant to be given as a gift between friends, to honor all my friendships around the world. I'm now writing four other books and hope to publish one or two in 2018. I hope they will contribute to this country that I love so much.

As a woman entrepreneur, I hope to inspire other women (both immigrants and others) to pursue and achieve their dreams. I hope to leave a positive legacy in the banking industry by helping many small financial institutions have a strong foundation. Lastly, I hope that through my speaking and writings, I will inspire many people to be the best they can be, follow their dreams, and never forget that God is the source of our hope and help. God is the one who has blessed America, and it is still the land of opportunity when you work hard and are willing to contribute to society.

MEDIA LINKS

greencardvoices.org/speakers/marci-malzahn

Garissa,
Kenya

Haji Yusuf

From: Garissa, Kenya (Somali)
Current City: St. Cloud, MN

Current Business:
Orange Oak Advertising
orangeoakmn.com

> "REGARDLESS OF WHERE WE COME FROM, WE SHARE SPACE TOGETHER."

I grew up in a small town in the northern part of Kenya called Garissa, which was mostly inhabited by Somali people after the coup. I grew up there from the late '80s onward—I attended an eight-year primary school in a community largely made up of very well-cultured Muslim people. It was just like in Somalia and many other places in Ethiopia.

My dad and mom passed away when I was very young, so I was raised by my brothers. I have twenty-two siblings. I have only one sibling from the same mother: my sister. My dad married a lot of wives; that's normal in Africa and other parts of the world. One of my siblings passed away a while back, so there are now twenty-one brothers and sisters back home in Africa. It's just my sister and I in America right now. Before she died, my mother was a small business owner, a small trader selling clothes in Kenya. She inspired me to become the entrepreneur I am today.

In the mornings we went to school, and in the evenings we went to the Madrasa to learn about religion. On the weekends we went out to the Tana, a beautiful river that passed by the town. When it was the rainy season, we would go farther into the open space, looking for places where the water collected and made for perfect swimming; it was a relief from the heat that came from Garissa's position along the equator. The mosquitos bit at night, but the cool breeze, the warm morning sunrise, and the bugs singing all the time were amazing.

Hundreds of kids would hang out in the evening, and there would be fights and jokes and fun. There would be a lot of intimidation and bullying, but it was just part of growing up; it was a sort of test for the young men, and the older ones too. That's what we did, unlike in America, where young people probably stay home, go out to the movies, or hang out at a park. For us, it was jumping off trees, swimming in small bodies of water, and hunting for bugs or wild animals close to where we lived. The whole village raised everyone. We knew each other like family. Everybody knew who I was, so if I did something bad, I would get reported on.

My childhood was beautiful. I would never want to trade growing up in Africa for anything. It was just an amazing experience for me.

The ethnic minority that I come from occupies parts of Kenya and has never been treated very well by the successive governments that arose from our nation's independence. My ethnic group was targeted with a lot of torture, killing, and disappearances in the early '60s because people from that group wanted to leave Kenya and become a part of Somalia. The government did not take that lightly, so they went around shooting and beating us even in the early '80s.

When I was young, my mom, my sister, and I were taken away from our home one morning by the Kenyan army. They took us and about six hundred others to a field—it was hot, with no shade and no water. They started questioning, caning, and beating us—I could hear people getting tortured from afar. It was a sad day, and it went on from eight in the morning until around two thirty, when the sun was right above us.

Luckily, my dad was politically well-connected. He came with my younger sister, identified us, and took us with him. But I know there were hundreds of families that were not so lucky that day, and they lost their lives. Extrajudicial killings and suppression were part of daily life, from the '80s til now.

Things have changed a little bit since then. Still, over the past fifty years, we've never had good schools. I used to be a little bit fearful when I was younger. But as I grew up and got a little bit older and braver, this fear motivated me—from when I first came to the States to this day. I don't want anyone in the community to be victimized by something like I was. That has partially influenced my leadership and who I am today.

I never thought I would come to the US. I used to watch Hollywood movies and had this idea that America was all powerful, that there were guys like Rambo and Chuck Norris who could take out a whole army. Hollywood movies about relationships and heroes and villains, those were the only ideas I had. In the movies they had hip-hop, they had women, they had cars, and it looked really wonderful. I never thought I would come to a place like that, but it happened that the very first school I got into gave me a visa to come study in Florida.

Flying over Chicago was amazing. At noon, the pilot told us, "Ladies and gentlemen, this is your pilot. On your left side is Lake Michigan. Lake Michigan is a warm water body . . ." As he talked about Lake Michigan and how beautiful it was, I was amazed. I asked the guy next to me what was on the ground.

He said, "That's snow. You've never seen snow before?" No, I never had, except in the movies. It was the stuff from Home Alone, which I used to watch a lot. *This is just what I see in the movies,* I thought.

We landed in Florida, and again I thought that this was just like the movies. But over the next few days, reality started sinking in. I realized it was not like the movies at all. Nothing was for free. You had to find papers, you had to work, you had to hustle, and you had to be a survivor. It proved to be too much; I wasn't able to complete my undergrad in Florida.

Luckily, I had some relatives in Minneapolis who told me to come. When I moved there, I couldn't work because I hadn't gotten all my paperwork yet. Because finding a job was very hard for me, I stayed with people who did have work. Some of them were relatives. It was tough; I was powerless because if they kicked me out, I would be homeless. Luckily, that didn't happen, and I could be much more comfortable. Everyone was connected in the Somali community—friends and families stayed together as they worked things out and waited for their paperwork to go through.

I've been in Minnesota since 2000. I started from nothing. When I finally got my paperwork, I got a job at Home Depot. I used to arrange wood outside along with the flowers. The lawnmowers usually came in containers, so I would unbox them. I would also get driven out to Wisconsin in the mornings to do manual handiwork and put stuff together, arriving back in Burnsville by four to go to Home Depot.

I also worked in the MSP airport for a used-car rental business. I would check cars in and out. I also worked as a security guard at the airport. I would stay there the whole night until morning doing those jobs. It wasn't fun. There were weekends when we would hang out as a community, but it was mostly jobs, jobs, jobs, jobs. I had to pay my bills and take care of everything as best as I could.

After getting more experience living in the States, I worked in customer service. I did collection hours as collection agent, calling people who were behind on their credit cards. I got some really weird and fun replies because of my accent. From that experience, finally, I got the opportunity to continue my studies, which I hadn't finished in Florida. My cousin worked at St. Cloud university and recommended that I enroll there; it has been my home ever since.

There were instances when I was renting an apartment and the rental manager, knowing that I wasn't from here, treated me differently from other renters. At some jobs, I wouldn't get a promotion even if I had the qualifications and experience, but I saw other people come in three months after me and end up as my managers. I want to make sure my son doesn't experience this—that he is treated equally, respected, and looked to for his character, not his skin color, his religion, or the place he comes from.

I have two kids, a boy and a girl. Spending time with them is very important to me. I also have a wife who I brought all the way from England. She is an amazing woman. She holds a master's in finance and is much smarter than me—I'm not smart, I'm just hard-working. There's a big difference.

Because of the the discrimination and brutality and mistreatment of my people, I tend to like to tell stories about what was going on. I always wanted to be a journalist; I had a camera when I was growing up, and people would call me Mohamin, after the famous cameraman from Africa who did the Ethiopian farmline way back in the '80s. He was Kenyan, and he died in a plane crash in Madagascar. I've always gravitated toward cameras, media, writing, and news. I like to shoot video and sit down to edit it. Some people like reading, and some people like writing books, but shooting and editing video is my hobby. I am passionate about getting the best shot.

I've come to love this country and its principles. Are we perfect as a country? No. Have we made mistakes? Yeah. We have some ugly history. But I feel that we learn from our mistakes. We have a bright future for this country when issues of racism and diversity are addressed. But that's not going to happen unless there's a struggle.

I've experienced racism in this country. I've experienced discrimination in this country. I've been treated very badly in this country. But I don't take those experiences with me. I take the experiences that have been more positive: the people who have been great and supported me, who have given me the opportunity to succeed. As an immigrant entrepreneur, I use that as motivation to do more for myself and for my family. That's what it comes down to.

A lot of people think that immigrants come here and get stuff for free, but nobody ever gave me stuff for free. I pay my rent. I took myself to school and bought my first car. I've never broken this country's laws. I've never stolen anything, contrary to the ideas people have about immigrants (especially around this most recent presidential election). I've never even gotten a speeding ticket. I'm living proof; you can go back and look at my history. You can see that I've been positive for myself, my family, and the people I represent in my community. I never judge someone unless they give me a reason to. It's not in my way to do that.

I've started two businesses: Orange Oak Media and Home Health Care. I've also created an organization together with Natalie Ringsmuth. We call it Unite Cloud, and through it we have contributed to conversations in our community about race, religion, sex—everything that makes us suspicious of each other and makes us look different from each other. We look at the things that unite us, things that we have in common. Regardless of where we come from, we share space together. We get to see each other on the bus, in traffic, in the shopping center, and at schools. So Unite Cloud helps to build relationships and ask how we are going to attract each other in those environments—as people, not as whites, blacks, Muslims, Christians, gays, lesbians. As people who have feelings, as people who have families, as people who care about this country, as people who love this country, as people who love their neighbors and understand who they are, as people who are not a threat to anyone but just want to make something out of themselves.

A big part of that conversation has been impactful; when I get messages in my inbox or on my phone from people who I've never met, when strangers recognize me, that tells me that I'm doing something right. When every media company in the world from Al Jazeera to CNN to the *New York Times* comes looking for me and Natalie, talking about what we are doing for this community, that tells me that I'm doing something for this country. It's the same dream that people before me in the African-American community had through slavery and the civil rights movement. Martin Luther King, Jr. opened the door for someone like me to speak today for other communities.

I got where I am today because I taught myself how to solve meaningful problems, and then practiced keeping things simple. What drives me as an entrepreneur is the service I can offer to people who are my customers, people around me, and the community that I come from. I've learned that you have to think outside the box, surround yourself with great talent, and then execute your plan. My advice would be to take risks, keep trying and evolving, and find a place in the cycle to connect.

I am not not Martin Luther King, Jr., I am not Mahatma Gandhi, and I am not Nelson Mandela, but I am a person and a friend and a neighbor and a husband and a community leader and somebody that cares about the St. Cloud community a lot. I have grown here and have called this place home. That is more important to me than anything else.

MEDIA LINKS

greencardvoices.org/speakers/haji-yusuf

Caracas,
Venezuela

Andrés A. Parra

From: Caracas, Venezuela
Current City: Minneapolis, MN

Current Business:
Venus Directions
venusdirections.com

> "IT'S ALMOST LIKE I WAS EXTRACTED AND MOVED AND THEN ALL THESE THINGS HAPPENED WITH ME ON THE OUTSIDE. IT SEEMS LIKE I MISSED THE LIVES OF MY RELATIVES AND FRIENDS AND THEY MISSED MINE."

I was born in Caracas, Venezuela, a city of about three or four million people. I lived in the suburbs. Small nuclear family. Nice, comfortable life. At the time, the city was very nice. It's inside a valley and has beautiful mountains that I hiked around a fair amount. I used to be in the Boy Scouts. The Caribbean Sea was really close by, so probably within an hour and a half we could be on the beach, which we did often.

I went to public school in Caracas. It was an experimental school; they tried new and improved teaching methods, educational tools, and whatnot. It was very well received, as far as the level of education and all that during the '70s and even the '80s. Later on it got a little sketchy for political and economic reasons, but it was still fun.

I had, and still have, lots of friends back in Venezuela; you know, those friendships that last a lifetime. Like I said, I lived in the suburbs, where there were a lot of new families. I used to run around with a whole bunch of little kids, and we would be gone from morning until afternoon or night, until somebody called for us to go eat. We never planned anything. We just grabbed our bikes or our skateboards, went out, and came back when the sun went down. It was very safe. We played a lot of different ball games like soccer or handball. Not necessarily organized handball like you would in a league or anything like that—no, we just found a wall and a rubber ball and started playing. We would grab the ball and throw it, rather than hit it with our hands like a racquet. I also played baseball in the street in between all of that. We would stop if a car went by, which was rare because we were in a neighborhood that didn't have a lot of traffic. We did a lot of that: bicycle riding, hiking, going to the beach.

At the time, it was idyllic; we could go into the city within ten minutes. Go downtown. Go to the open markets. We had interesting services and people came to our neighborhoods because we were further removed from the city; for example, bakeries were usually run by people from Portugal. Restaurants by and large were run by people either from Italy or from Spain, and they would cluster in different parts of the city too.

People from Portugal would come around in a Vespa, the little motorcycle. And they would have a little harmonica, and you would hear the sound and know that was the guy sharpening your kitchen knives. They would come around, put the Vespa down, rest it on the kickstand, put a belt around the back wheel, and grab your knives and sharpen them right then and there. We also had people who would come and shine shoes, so parents would put their shoes outside on the front step and a guy—usually from Venezuela, but from the not-so-affluent part of the city—would come in and do the shining. They would stay there for an hour and shine everybody's shoes, it was that kind of a thing.

We had the donut guy—he would come in a little car and open the trunk and there would be fresh donuts. There was the ice cream man. There was, and this was particularly great, the horse guy. He would come in with five or six horses, and you would pay the equivalent of a dime for a half-hour ride or twenty cents for a full hour. The more you did that, if he knew how well you did on a horse, he would let you run with it. This was all over blacktop, not like in the country or anything like that.

We had a lot of that. I never heard of that existing anywhere, in any other country.

We all went to kindergarten through high school in the same school. So that was convenient and very familiar. We were always looking forward, switching buildings after we graduated grades.

We also became very familiar with our bus drivers. They became more like family than just the bus drivers who came and picked us up. The particular service that we had would have field trips on a Saturday. They didn't have to. They were not associated with the school or anything, but they would say, "If you want to go to a park, let's make it a day." So they would pick up all the kids they would regularly pick up on a school week and take us out to a park, and we would spend the day. We became a family and grew up that way. To this day, I still know where those bus drivers are in the world. That must be forty years ago by now.

Everything was very easygoing. We would visit friends that lived close by. We didn't plan visits for the most part; we would just drop by and stay for dinner. There wasn't a formal invitation; you just went there and were expected to eat there. Even if you went home and ate again, that was okay. It was all very easygoing, without very much formality.

I have always had an affinity for the US, as far as my taste in music, clothing, and those sorts of things are concerned. I've always been good at languages, and English came to me fairly easily, or at least easier than it did to my classmates. Toward the end of high school there was a trend: after you finished high school, you would spend a year elsewhere. For the most part, it was here in the US. You would go through and repeat your last year of high school in the US. I didn't go through that process because I applied too late, but I did find something similar; I went to Barbados and studied for six months. I went as an exchange student and liked it, so I learned British English before I learned American English, plus the local dialect, Bajan. You can think of it as British English with a Spanish accent; it's a little bit thick.

That whetted my appetite for travel. After I went back to Venezuela, there was an opportunity: university! I had been an above-average student in high school but for some reason at university I wasn't doing quite as well as I thought I would be. There was an opportunity at the time—a scholarship program sponsored by the government. They would send students to different parts of the world to study for certain careers. I applied for mechanical engineering because at the time it seemed they wanted attorneys, engineers, or perhaps professors—something of substance rather than the arts. At least that's what I thought; I wasn't explicitly told that.

While I waited to hear back about my application, I was working. There was a period when I needed to do something; even though I didn't necessarily need to work right after school, that was just our culture. You really didn't move out of your home until you got married, and sometimes not even then; you brought your wife in, or your husband, and became a bigger family. But I was a little restless and wanted to work, so I started looking for something to do and worked as a bank teller. That lasted a couple of months, and I then I got bored. Then, I worked in a manufacturing company doing assembly—that lasted a week, so I wasn't being very consistent.

At that point, an acquaintance of mine who worked at a film production company said, "You know, we're looking for an assistant, a 'gofer.'" So I said, "Well, that sounds like me." I went in, interviewed, and became an assistant. They did a lot of national commercials. At the time, we were still working on 35mm film. I got a taste of all that and became really connected with my boss. He became my manager, my mentor. I became an associate producer, and then I became a cameraman, then started doing some more lighting, and so on and so forth.

I was fortunate enough to be accepted into the program, so I quit that job. When I moved here and was going through college, I still worked as a cameraman on a freelance basis.

At first, the program told me I was going to go to Canada, and I went, "Well, great, I will go to Canada." It was supposed to be for the entire length of the studies; then you would go back and work for the government for a couple of years in your chosen field, and then you were released from your obligations. About a month before I had to leave the country, they changed the plans and told me I wasn't going to Canada; I was going to the US. Either one would have been fine.

Interestingly enough, I did really well at college here, taking the same subjects that I did back in Venezuela. I don't know why, but it happened. I was in a groove and went for mechanical engineering undergrad. I graduated in three years because high school in Venezuela was a little more advanced than high school here in the US—we graduated two years earlier, when we were sixteen. I tested out of generals here, which shaved some time off my university career.

I finished my undergrad career, went back to Venezuela, and presented my papers. However, they didn't have a place for me, so they released me from my obligations. I decided that I needed to come back to the States and get some filmmaking production credentials. I also decided that I was going to look for a master's somewhere. I couldn't find any teaching assistantships or scholarships to go to for my master's in the arts, so I changed my thinking a little bit and went for a master's in mass communication in the US. After my first semester there, I received a teaching assistantship and also worked as a cameraman on the local campus cable station. That period lasted about a year and half.

When I finished my master's, that's kind of where life really started. I moved out of college and didn't know what to do. I had freelanced as a cameraman during college and had done a lot of sports coverage, so I continued doing that. Then I started moving into some commercial shooting, and then some corporate shooting. I moved from where I was in Ohio to Pennsylvania, and then upstate New York, and then, eventually, Minneapolis.

I didn't set out to be an entrepreneur. I was working for a production company, and I realized that I was working too hard for the salary I was receiving. So I talked to a coworker who was getting ready to go freelance, and he offered me a retainer situation, the perfect bridge between occupying a staff position and being a full freelancer. We worked together for about a year, and then I decided I could go completely on my own after having built a clientele that liked working with me.

I am fortunate to be very versatile; I can work in different capacities within the film and A/V industry. I think one of the main things to remember when you're in business for yourself is to be flexible and provide the best customer service. Being in my industry requires me to be, if not proficient, definitely aware of what is available and new in the market. Staying relevant is extremely important and cultivating your existing clients will provide you with a vast and rich pool from which to draw when it comes to acquiring new projects. Talk to other business owners in your industry. You'd be surprised how willing people are to talk about their businesses.

I believe that people need to like who they work with. I know from what my clients tell me that they enjoy working with me. Of course, one needs to provide the service that clients need and then go above and beyond. I have decided not to let cultural or immigration issues get to me, and I don't believe that I have had any hardships based on my race or immigrant status. There have been opportunities available to me as an immigrant to present my services to potential clients and get their business; however, I have not based my success as an entrepreneur solely on my status as an immigrant.

Although I gave up a few things in order to live in the United States, I have had a great, fruitful life. I've been successful to the point that I have now, for the the last ten years, been able to help my family back in Venezuela. This is exceptional given the turns of events in the country's economy, politics, and so forth. But I've had to give up the day-to-day interaction that we have there, which in my view is because of the culture. In Venezuela the culture is a little warmer, there is a little more interaction. I've had to give up growing up with my high school friends or family. It's almost like I was extracted and moved, and all these things have happened with me on the outside. It seems like I missed the lives of my relatives and friends and they missed mine.

Being with family more often is something that I have also had to give up. It's better now because of social media, but the first twenty years were a little harder. We didn't have smartphones or the Internet. I don't write a lot, so I wasn't in touch with my family via mail. At the same time, I created a family here. I have two beautiful daughters—Lexi, who will graduate high school in 2018, and Alyssa, who is a sophomore in college. Both of them are involved with their friends and their own pursuits. I created a business that is still going, and I am able to further my career. Back in Venezuela right now, or in the last fifteen years, it probably would have been harder due to politics and the economy.

I'm trying to keep up with what I need to learn for my business—for example, technology. I love to ride motorcycles, I love to travel, I love to go to movies, and I love living in a city that is so cosmopolitan. I know the four corners of both St. Paul and Minneapolis. My existence is just enjoying that and seeing where life takes me tomorrow.

I try to show Minnesotans what a Venezuelan is like in terms of work ethic and human interaction. I work with many different people often, and I'm able to relate my experiences of where I'm from. People see and hear me and say something like, "Well, you don't look Mexican." I don't want to say I educate, but I definitely show that there are differences between Venezeulans, Guatemalens, Nicaraguans, Costa Ricans, and Mexicans. My two girls also have that dual understanding; I think that perpetuates through generations, and they're able to disseminate or propagate that kind of knowledge in their everyday life. I think that's my main contribution, if any.

Some lessons I've learned: Listen to your client. Provide alternatives when your client's expectations are beyond their reach. Look for ways to provide excellent service without cutting corners. Be honest. Work from a place of abundance rather than a place of scarcity. And network, network, network.

MEDIA LINKS

greencardvoices.org/speakers/andres-a-parra

New Delhi,
India

nize that I do not have all the answers. Do not be reluctant to ask for help. For every refusal, you will get someone who is ready to assist you.

I think I've added to the long stream of very lustrous, hard working, wonderful people who came before me and who will come after me, because today there is more mobility around the world. Talent is universal. People are going back and forth. I hope that in adding to that stream of talent I've made it more like a river, worthy of the Mississippi born in our state. That is what I would call my contribution; going forward, if I can build on this contribution, I'd be happy to.

There are many who were there for me when I left for my journey and came here. I would like to thank them all, and I would like to also say that I am trying to give back to others. Working with Xavier is one such way. Having a business, being an entrepreneur, is another way to be inclusive and to give back what I got over the years from different people: complete strangers, friends, family members, colleagues, neighbors, and just the regular Joe on the street.

MEDIA LINKS

greencardvoices.org/speakers/ameeta-jaiswal-dale

Ho Chi Minh City,
Vietnam

Wanny Huynh

From: Ho Chi Minh City, Vietnam
Current City: Minneapolis, MN

Current Business:
Wanny Huynh International
wannyhuynh.com

> "I BEGAN TO GROW FINANCIALLY. I BOUGHT A BIGGER HOUSE AND A FANCY CAR. I WAS LIVING THE DREAM OF WHAT I THOUGHT A SUCCESSFUL BUSINESS MAN SHOULD LOOK LIKE. A FEW YEARS INTO IT, THOUGH, THE MARKET CRASHED. I ENDED UP LOSING EVERYTHING: MY BIG HOUSE, MY FANCY CAR.."

When I was eight years old, my family escaped Vietnam on foot, hoping to make it to the free world. From 1975 to the early '80s, two million Vietnamese attempted to escape Vietnam. Out of those, only eight hundred thousand made it to refugee camps. Our family was one of the lucky few who made it to a refugee camp alive, but it didn't come without a price. There were many challenges and obstacles on our path as we journeyed through Cambodia to Thailand.

One of those obstacles was crossing the checkpoints. Each checkpoint was guarded by half a dozen of the Khmer Rouge, armed with shotguns and rifles. They would search us up and down to make sure we didn't have anything valuable on us, taking whatever they could find before they let us through.

Finally, at the fourth checkpoint, we had nothing left but the clothes on our backs. After searching each one of us and finding nothing, the guards decided to wave our family through. My mom was carrying my five-month old baby sister and my older cousin was carrying my other sister, who was five years old; my brother and I followed closely behind.

Just when we thought we were safe, we heard a voice: "Wait. The two boys stay." The soldiers grabbed my brother and me.

My mom begged and cried for the soldiers to let her two boys go, but they did not give in and held us tightly in their arms. My mom continued to beg and cry, "Please let my two boys go!" One of the soldiers finally had enough of this. He pulled out his handgun and fired—bam, bam, bam!

The bullets came inches from hitting her face, piercing through her hair and clothing. A few passersby saw all of this. They feared for my mom's life and their own. Two younger gentlemen quickly rushed over, grabbed my mom by the arms, and dragged her along the path. My brother and I, ten and eight years old, got held back by the Khmer Rouge.

Long after our family had journeyed on, the soldiers didn't know what to do with us. Finally, they decided to let us go. The only thing we could think to do was to follow the path that our family was traveling. My brother and I continued down the path through the open, grassy fields of Cambodia in the middle of the night. The only light that guided us was the full moon up above.

Halfway through our journey, we stopped. We looked at each other and didn't know what to do. The only thing we could think of was to return to the checkpoint, hoping that our family would return for us. That was a huge mistake.

When we arrived back at the checkpoint, we ran into another group of soldiers who had come to take over the checkpoint. One of the leaders saw us and took us back home with him. We discovered later that he wanted a son in his family because all he had were two young girls. He treated us nice when he was around; he would feed and play with us. His wife was the opposite. When her husband was off for duty, she began to put us to work. She made my brother and me carry heavy loads of rice bags back and forth from the house to the street market, where she would sell them. When we weren't doing that, she made us carry heavy pails of water from the well into the house. At night she made us sleep outside without a mosquito net. Every morning, my brother and I woke up to dozens and dozens of mosquito bites all over our skinny bodies. Every day I wondered if we would ever see our family again.

Meanwhile, in a town nearby, my mom had not given up hope. Every day, she sought out travelers and asked them if anyone had seen her two missing boys. Many stepped up and said, "Yeah, we have seen your two boys. Give us money, and we will bring the boys back to you." My mother gave them money, then waited and waited, but there was no sign of her two boys. Still, she persisted, continuing to ask anyone who she came across if they had seen her boys. Day after day, week after week, my mom went out and searched for any information of our whereabouts, only to face disappointment.

One day, a young lady who happened to be traveling between towns heard that my mom was looking for two little boys. Out of curiosity, she approached my mom and said, "Auntie, the two boys you're looking for . . ." She began to describe two boys to my mom. After being scammed many times, my mom wasn't about to be tricked again.

Then the lady described the black mole on my upper lip, and that grabbed my mom's attention. The young lady went on to describe the clothes that we were wearing, and my mom was finally convinced that she was telling the truth. She finally coughed out a sentence: "Would you take me to them?" After two months of being apart from our family, we were finally reunited. My mom said, "If you continued to walk another half a mile, you would have run into the family." You see, my brother and I came close, but we couldn't see the results. The lesson I learned from this and have carried with me to this day is to never, ever give up.

During our stay in that small town, war was still going on between Vietnam and Cambodia. The next thing we knew, our family was in the middle of the battlefield with bullets and missiles flying over our heads. We sought shelter in a nearby bunker. Then we heard a loud voice: "Move your family away from here!" We all looked. There was this older gentleman in his mid-sixties who was warning us to get away from that bunker. My mom didn't think twice. She gathered all of us, and we began to make our way to find a new location.

Twenty yards away, we found a new bunker. We then noticed that the old man had jumped into the same bunker he just warned us about. A few seconds later—boom! A missile landed in his bunker. That old man saved our lives.

After surviving the battlefield, our family settled in a refugee camp in Thailand for two years before we got someone to sponsor us to come to America. Our family arrived in Minnesota in the winter of '84. The temperature was below zero. After stepping foot off the plane into MSP international airport, the first thing to welcome me was the chill that hit my face.

We settled in a small town called Faribault. During our first winter, we had to walk to school; we didn't know anything about the bus system. The school was about a mile away from home. Snow was up to our neck, and the temperature was below zero.

One cold day, my older brother, sister, and I were walking to school when we heard a car horn. We were very happy to see that the man behind the wheel was one of our neighbors. "You need a ride?" he asked. Before we could answer him, all three of us were already in the back seat of his car. He had saved us from the freezing temperature. But we weren't safe yet—we came face to face with a steep hill. The car tried to go up the hill, but the snow and the icy road forced us down. Every two feet we climbed, we ended up sliding back four feet.

I didn't want to get out and walk in the cold weather. I begin to pray, "God, please help this car make it up this steep hill; it's cold and we don't want to walk." God must have heard my call, because the car slowly began to make its way up the hill. What a big relief.

The cold was one of the culture shocks I experienced. Then there was the language barrier. Arriving in America at ten years old, all I knew was "A-B-C" and "1-2-3." I was thrown into second grade, and I couldn't understand what the teacher was saying. I couldn't communicate with the others students. So I turned to what I knew best: the TV. I began watching Sesame Street. Soon I began to pick up a few words here and there. I began to have hope, hope that I could learn this new language.

Up until high school, I didn't have a clue as to what I wanted to do with my life. Then I came across the movie Pretty Woman. The character played by Richard Gere was a successful businessman. He was always surrounded by beautiful women, driving fancy cars, and dressed in fine clothes. I was like, "I want to do that! I want to be like him!"

But my parents had a different plan for me. They gave me four choices: become a doctor, lawyer, accountant, or engineer. I was terrible at math, so engineer and accountant were out the door. I couldn't defend myself in court, so lawyer was out too. The only thing left was "doctor." "Doctor Huynh" sounded kind of cool, so off I went to study medicine.

A year and a half later, I dropped out. I realized being in the medical field was not something I wanted to do with my life; I had done it just to please my parents. My heart wasn't in school anymore. I ended up dropping out because I wasn't doing what I was passionate about.

I moved back to my parents' basement. One day, a buddy of mine from high school called me up and said, "Wanny, you need to come out and listen to this guy speak. It will change your life." I had two choices: I could either stay home and watch the rerun of Gilligan's Island, or I could go listen to some guy speak. The choice was clear, so off I went.

Next thing I knew, I was in a room of about three hundred people. On the stage was a man in a three-piece suit. The only reason I stuck around was that the man onstage reminded me of Richard Gere, a successful businessman. Halfway through his talk, he said something that was very moving, very inspiring. I began getting goosebumps all over my body. At that moment, he awakened the sleeping giant. I had found my true calling. I told myself, "I want to do that; I want to get on stage and inspire other people the way he inspired me."

I didn't know anything about the speaking business; I didn't have a mentor or a coach to turn to. I put the thought of becoming an inspirational speaker aside and began to pursue a sales career—after all, I wanted to become an international businessman like Richard Gere. I joined network marketing groups hoping to get rich quick. I sold everything from kitchen knives to water filters to financial products. I failed in all of these endeavors. But it all allowed me to step outside of my comfort zone. I gained new confidence and I learned how to deal with rejection.

I realized sales wasn't for me, so I quit and ended up getting a part-time job loading containers for UPS at the Minneapolis–St. Paul International Airport. One day during my break, a coworker mentioned to me that she also worked for the airline part time. She begin sharing with me all the perks and benefits she was getting while working for the airline. She shared with me that I could fly first and business class anywhere I wanted for little to nothing. I was sold. I put in my application, and a few weeks later I got called for the interview. It helped that I had some sales background, because that meant I was able to sell myself during the interview. I think that was one of the reasons I got hired.

Within the first year, I traveled to many exotic places such as Hong Kong, Singapore, Hawaii, and Thailand. During my flights, I got to sit in first and business class; my seatmates were CEOs of major corporations, entrepreneurs, and businessmen, people I wanted to be like. I began to pick their brains. I acted like they acted, dressed the way they dressed, and read the same books that they were reading. One day someone recommended a book by Robert Kiyosaki, Rich Dad Poor Dad. I began to read it follow its principles. I got into real estate part time while still working for the airline. The next thing I knew, money was coming in so easily for me that I decided to quit my the airline and get into real estate full time.

I began to grow financially. I bought a bigger house and a fancy car. I was living the dream of what I thought a successful business man should look like. A few years into it, though, the market crashed. I ended up losing everything: my big house, my fancy car.

One day I found myself beaten, broken, and homeless, sitting in the broken-down car I had bought from my friend for a thousand dollars. I couldn't even afford to pay him at that time. He told me to just keep it and pay him back when I had the money. The car had a mile-long list of problems that came with it—I prayed to God every day to please get me from point A to point B safely.

Sitting in that broken-down car on a hot summer day, I saw a Caribou Coffee in front of me. I couldn't afford to buy a cup of ice that day. I reached into my pocket and pulled out my last dollar bill. I asked myself an important question: "How do I turn this dollar bill into a million dollars?" As I looked up, I saw a big, green sign in the corner of my eye. It read Dollar Tree.

With my last dollar in my hand, I marched over to the Dollar Tree. A few minutes later, I walked out with a composite notebook in my hand. On the front page, I wrote "Journey to financial freedom." I turned the page and began writing down questions: "Why am I broke? Who do I need to be to get myself out of this mess?" Surprisingly, answers started pouring into me, as if God were speaking to me. I couldn't write them down fast enough.

That day marked a turning point in my life. I began to dig deep inside and discover my true passion. Earlier, I mentioned that I wanted to be a inspirational speaker. It took a big downward turn for me to find my true calling. Eighteen years after that first desire, I began to pursue what I was passionate about: public speaking, sharing ideas with people, and telling stories to inspire and uplift. Once I knew what I wanted to do, the how became very easy.

I joined Toastmasters and begin speaking at every opportunity that I could get. I began to network with like-minded people. I began to grow in my personal development and my speaking skills. I went out and published four books. Two of them made it to the Amazon bestsellers list. I've spoken at major corporations such as 3M, Blue Cross Blue Shield, and many others.

One thing I have learned along the way is that for you to be successful, you need a mentor or a coach, someone to help guide you along your path. You can start by finding someone who is already doing the thing that you want to do and asking them to mentor you—I spent eighteen years running around in circles because I didn't have a mentor or a coach. Make sure to surround yourself with like-minded people. And start networking with others, because you never know who you might run into.

MEDIA LINKS

greencardvoices.org/speakers/wanny-huynh

Santurce,
Puerto Rico

José Figueroa

From: Santurce, Puerto Rico
Current City: St. Paul, MN

Current Business:
Raven Studios
ravenstudios.net

> "I HOPE TO BRING MINNESOTA SOME INTERESTING ART, ART THAT IS VERY MULTICULTURAL AND VERY DIVERSIFIED."

My three brothers and I were born in Puerto Rico and raised by my mom and dad. At one point, everyone but me moved to New York City, leaving me in Puerto Rico with my grandmother and grandfather. They raised me until the age of ten or twelve.

In Puerto Rico, I was like Mowgli in *The Jungle Book*. I liked to climb mango trees, all the time, and nature was part of who I was. My grandfather and my grandmother were interesting people. My grandmother is what was called a *curandera*. A *curandera* is almost like a priestess, someone who understands herbs and healing. Being a healer was a very important part of her. I took part in some ceremonies, and I did all the dances that were part of our culture.

What people don't understand about the culture in Puerto Rico is that there are three demographic groups. The indigenous people of the island are called the Taíno. They were there before it was called Puerto Rico, "Rich Port." That name came from the Spaniards when they invaded and enslaved the Taínos to join the African slaves they had brought to mine gold—the island's original name was Borinquen. A person who was born and raised on the island has a certain type of Latin pride. When someone from another Latin country asks us where we are from, we say, "Yo soy Boricua." They know immediately that we're from Puerto Rico.

I gravitated to the indigenous part of the island because my grandmother was of that faction. She was a Taína, and my grandfather was black. Carolina is a part of the island where everyone is black or we call them Trigueño, like Harlem. Then you have the Ponce part of the island, where everyone is fair-skinned with blond hair and blue eyes. My dad came from that side of the island. He was of Spanish descent and came from a long line of conquistadors.

I was Catholic—by birth, not by choice. Later I discovered the atrocities from when the Spanish invaded Puerto Rico, the horrible things they did to the Taínos and the African slaves. I was very close to my mother's side, which was Africa-centric and very indigenous in their practices. I have a love and passion for Santeria. Santeria is connected to the curanderos—it's basically a way that the people of the island were able to hide their religion in plain sight from the Spanish conquistadors. The Spanish were enforcing Catholicism on the people of the island, but the Taínos and the Africans had their own gods to pray to. So they said, "How can we hide this?" They mixed the Catholic deities with the African and Taíno deities. That later became Santeria. It's its own universe.

I was part of a lot of ceremonies, and I've seen some pretty fascinating things. One of my aunties was taken over by Chango, a very powerful deity. If I had to describe her, I would say she looks like Aunt Jemima with her hands on her hips, a very proud black woman. Her mirror image, the Catholic component, would be Santa Barbara. Santa Barbara has very fair skin, red hair, a crown, a red-and-white cape, and a giant sword in front of her. They are complete opposites—the yin and the yang of that deity. I found the whole ceremonial part of my life so fascinating because it was not what you would find in a Catholic Church, where it is so quiet, and people worship in a certain way. When we worshipped, there was music and dance. There was drumming, and it was full of vibrant activity. That was what my grandmother surrounded me with on the island when I was growing up. I found great solace in that.

I realized years later that my grandfather ran numbers. It wasn't exactly like the mob, but he was like a don. When people bet on horses and things, he took their bets. I noticed that he had this little notebook, and people would shout "Don Miguel!" to him. He had this bravado and coolness to him. Everybody in the village loved him.

I became as I am through my connection to my grandparents. When I was told that my mom had sent for me, my first reaction was, "Why? I want to stay here with you, Grandma."

"But your family is all there in New York. Your brothers, don't you want to see your brothers?"

"Yeah, I want to see my brothers, but can I come back?"

And she said, "No, once you go to New York, you have to stay there with your family."

When I left the island, my grandmother and her troupe of friends collectively did a little ceremony for me. They sang a song called "En Mi Viejo San Juan," which means "in my old San Juan." It's a very beautiful ballad, and I remember that moment really, really clearly. It stood out in my mind. Every time I hear that song, it reminds me of that moment.

Moving to New York was bittersweet because I loved the island and I loved my grandparents. My mom and dad had sent for me because they thought I should be living with them and my brothers. When I came to New York City, it was winter, and I had never known what the cold was like. I touched snow for the very first time and thought, "*This is crazy.*"

I lived with my mom and dad for eight years. Then my grandmother moved to New York and got a place on 116th Street in Spanish Harlem. I moved in with her again for five years and got to tap back into my Latino roots.

I didn't speak English at all when I got to the States. I had to use my mom and dad, who had very poor command of English. They knew a little bit, but not enough. I couldn't even speak to my brothers because they didn't speak Spanish and I didn't speak English. Eventually, within a year, I learned enough English to be able to have conversations with my brothers. Even then, I was a bit of an embarrassment to them, because I spoke with a heavy accent. When people would ask them, "Is that your brother?" they would say, "Uh, no!" It was harsh. But not speaking the language as a kid toughened me up. I had to work harder than the next guy to get to a place where I could make my voice heard become part of the group.

Eventually we all became really close. My youngest brother, God rest his soul, he and I were actually very close. We were like Heckle and Jeckle; people called us the Bobbsey Twins. We looked nothing alike, but we dressed the same. Whenever we went to a new school, we always made sure we got outfits that matched so people knew we were brothers. I was very dark-skinned and he was very fair-skinned, so we wanted to make sure people knew we were the same, that we were from the same family. I'm the only one in the family who came out dark.

When my father passed away, we buried him on the Island. It was heartwarming to see my grandfather and grandmother again, because I could tell they'd never forgotten that they'd raised me and they were happy with the way I turned out.

I would say that my main obstacles as an immigrant were learning the language and assimilating into the culture. I think those two things really made me feel inadequate—I felt like I couldn't "hang," so to speak. Kids are really cruel, and they would ridicule me because I couldn't speak English well. It was really jarring for me. Once I was able to assimilate and became articulate in the language, I felt a sense of confidence that I didn't have before, but I never let go of my Latin roots.

I made sure I kept up with Spanish. I wanted to be able to speak, read, and write the language fluently and to hopefully pass it on to my kids. My daughters don't speak Spanish, but they understand it. I force them to try to speak Spanish, even though they hate it and are embarrassed because they can't pronounce certain words. I say, "Don't be embarrassed; that's how you learn. You've got to speak it." I'm very proud of my girls. They've turned out really, really well in their own ways. Each of them has gone in a different direction.

At one point, I changed my name because I was embarrassed by "Jose." That was really a turning point in my life. My high school coach and gymnastics teacher said, "Why do you call yourself 'Joe'? Isn't your name Jose?"

I replied, "Yeah, but I just find it easier for others to pronounce. People say Ho-ZAY, and that's wrong. It's actually pronounced Ho-SEH. So if you're going to pronounce it wrong, say Joe or Joseph." It never stuck. People just called me Jose. People would sing "Jose, can you see," to the tune of the Star-Spangled Banner. It got old real quick, and I got into fistfights over this stuff. Once I got out of high school, though, I was very balanced. I felt very secure in myself and who I was. I always pushed the Latino envelope.

High school was really where I found what I wanted in my life, and this was because of a gymnastics teacher named Richard Gallo. He was a very smart teacher. He really knew how to engage young people—not like any of the other teachers in the building. He was the one I emulated, because he loved what he did. I told him that I wanted to be a gymnast, that I wanted to compete in the Olympics. He looked at me and asked, "Are you really serious?" and I said, "Yeah." He told me all the steps that I needed to take.

I remember him giving me some really sound advice before I graduated. He said, "When you choose a career, choose something that you'd be willing to do for free but that you want to get paid for." This really resonated with me, and I stuck with it. I went to college—not because I wanted to be educated but because I wanted to be a varsity gymnast. That's the only way you can get into the Olympics. It took me from 1985 till 1996 to get my degree. In the meantime, I was a gymnast and a coach—I put twelve years into this sport. I never made it to the Olympics team, but I put two kids I was coaching onto the Junior Olympics team. I feel like I achieved what I set out to do, even though it wasn't for me personally.

In the middle of this, I discovered martial arts, and it is what shaped the rest of my life. The reason I'd wanted to do gymnastics in the first place was that I saw these Jackie Chan movies, and all the flipping and acrobatic stuff really appealed to me. My first experience with karate, I came in really cocky—thinking I was Bruce Lee, jumping up and down. They put me in the ring with a green belt. I'll never forget this guy; he laid me out in one shot. We began fighting, and he landed a punch to the chest that hit me so hard I couldn't breathe. I was on the floor sucking in wind. I could not believe someone could hit you that hard. I wanted to quit on that day, day one. I was like, "This is not for me." But then the master said to me, "Toughen up. Suck it up." I ended up staying in the school until I was a brown belt. I then started to find little bits and pieces of martial arts.

When I discovered Chinese martial arts, that's where the rest of my focus landed, tai chi particularly. Most people who study tai chi understand that it is a kind of meditation, very slow but very beautiful art. That was the way I saw it, anyway, but I was introduced to it very differently by a guy named Master Derick Trent, who was a young tai chi master. His teacher was named J. B. Lapuppet. He was teaching a hybrid form of martial arts using tai chi only as a foundation.

I thought the fast stuff was really cool, and I was really good at it—I won national titles in that art. But what I was really interested in and intrigued by was the slow stuff, the traditional tai chi, because it looked so mysterious. My teacher would smile and say "Oh, you don't want to learn this." I would say, "Oh yeah, I want to learn it."

He said my first lesson was to get to Manhattan by six in the morning. I lived in the Bronx and I had no car, so I took the bus at three in the morning. I got there at five past six, and he was eating his apple, looking at his watch. He said, "You're late." I tried to give him an excuse as to why I was late. He said, "Go home," turned around, and went back upstairs. The next day, I arrived earlier than he did. He said, "Okay, we can begin."

The first lesson was patience. He told me to do a movement, and then he would have me repeat it twenty or thirty times. I eventually got to the right speed, and within a few years I had become proficient in this style.

I discovered years later that the style I was learning was a hybrid. I was really searching for something more pure, more traditional. The Chen family style is the oldest form of tai chi, and was created four hundred years ago. I was very lucky that I came at the right time and the right place. My teacher, Master Ren Guang-Yi, came to this country straight from China in 1991. I became a disciple of his and have been with him for over twenty years.

He was very accepting. The makeup of his school was very interesting. It wasn't just Asian or just white; it was a mixture of people. I was the only Hispanic guy, and my teacher didn't understand what that was. I tried explaining Puerto Rico with the help of one of my kung fu brothers, Francis, who translated to Chinese.

Francis also told him that Puerto Ricans are known to be gang members that they carry switchblades and are from the Bronx. He wasn't completely wrong. I was in gangs as a youth. I've had my share of guns pointed in my face. I dodged a bullet once, from a .22-caliber rifle that was held to my face. Not knowing it was loaded, I knocked my hand across it, and the bullet went off. I lost a lot of hair and the hearing in my right ear for months. That was me as a teenage kid, trying to find myself. The gang stuff was seductive; it let me be part of a clique.

In 1995, my teacher certified me and my three other brothers from the school. We were four of his first-generation American disciples under the Chen family. We were recognized by the people in China. It is a really cool group because one of us was Asian, one Italian, one Puerto Rican, and the other one biracial, half Jewish and half Jamaican. I loved the fact that we were such a diverse group of guys. We all had our different backgrounds, but we brought our families together and were able to immerse ourselves in one culture. That is one of the things I loved about being around my teacher.

Now, mind you, martial arts put an enormous amount of stress on my family life because I was married and had children. I was really pushing the envelope, doing a lot of competitions and tournaments. In my competing days, I became a seven-time national champion and was inducted into three halls of fame. I produced some instructional videos on the subject of tai chi and wrote three books on the subject. At one point, as I got further along in my training, my teacher officially said I could go on my own. I eventually became a teacher myself. Stephan Berwick, my tai chi brother and cowriter on my book projects, was the one who focused my direction as a full-time tai chi teacher and eventually as a filmmaker. His influence to this date still motivates me to do my personal best.

I went to City College of New York and got a BS in physical education. I used that degree to do something very innovative with New York City schools. I introduced tai chi as the core curriculum for physical educations in two schools—one was in the south Bronx, a really tough school called Movement Education. Three years later, I went to a place in Manhattan called Manhattan School for Children and taught the curriculum. I did a really cool program with young kids, but it was a lot of work. By 1997, I was burned out because I was teaching tai chi by myself. It had become exhausting.

I then discovered theater through my kung fu brother Stephan. He introduced me to Fred Ho, who was doing a show at Erin Davis Hall in City College New York. It was a reading for a martial arts production called *Warrior Sisters*. This was a really fascinating piece of work, because the guy who wrote it was Asian American. He fused Asian music, jazz, and contemporary music together into performance art. This was his way of fusing martial arts with theater. It was the first show I ever saw like that. Fred Ho hired me, and from 1997 to 2004, I worked full-time as a choreographer for theatrical productions.

I worked several productions, which started by going on a national tour with Fred Ho's company. That put a strain on the family—I was away for three months. We toured forty-two cities. It was the most phenomenal experience ever. I learned so much as a producer, as a manager. Not only was I the choreographer, but I was also a character, an actor in the story.

Eventually, I retired from theater and went to film school at New York Film Academy for a one-year course on digital filmmaking. From there, I was able to form a company called Raven Studios, which was my attempt to do more martial arts films. From 2004 until today, I've managed to develop a modest production company that has produced multiple feature films, short films, and other projects that I am very proud of. I found working for myself was a bit more liberating than touring.

The constant hustle of finding jobs and clients has been the worst part. It's feast or famine when you work for yourself, but I wouldn't have it any other way. I've learned that I have to create my own contracts and nondisclosure agreements prior to doing any business. This keeps everyone honest, and I've found that business will flourish when trust is established upfront. It takes patience. Keep working on your craft and improving yourself. Be introspective and mindful in those quiet moments that shape your path toward enlightenment.

One of the projects I worked on involved the late Lou Reed, God rest his soul. Lou was learning tai chi from my master and had a real love for the art, as Stephan and I did. Somewhere along the line, we all came up with the idea of writing this script for a short film called "Final Weapon". The film was showcased in Minnesota and did very well in the local film festival. Before Lou passed away, there was talk of doing a feature film in Minnesota; after he passed away, we began to raise funds and awareness about this film. We want to make sure that it is a legacy to honor Lou Reed's memory.

I came to Minnesota because I met someone; I came specifically for that relationship. I hung up all my film stuff, and I dug 150 percent into my tai chi. That was how I made my money. I shelved the film project for some time, then dusted it off and did a little more, then put it away again. Recently, I finally finished wrapping up the film, but it took me a long time to put it together because I didn't have investors and was doing it all on my own. The nice thing about the project is that it really shines a light on all the collective experiences I've had. I am very close to my native culture, the Tíano. I wanted to do a story that really involved that part of my life.

I met someone in Minnesota who is like a brother now. His name is Larry Yasi, and he is of the Meskwaki nation. The Meskwaki are of the Wolf clan, and my spirit animal has always been a wolf. I never told him that. In addition to doing the film, he and I had a comic book that we started working on. It was composed by a young group of talented artists from Minnesota—I hired a guy name Beau Wilkens and his team to produce the comic book version of the movie. It started by accident—he did the storyboards for the movie, and they were so good that we agreed to adapt them into a graphic novel. The goal, again, is to bring awareness to the comic book and film, and what they're trying to do is showcase Minnesota as one of the characters in the story. The entire story takes place in Minnesota.

What I love about this project is that it's a very multicultural piece. It includes people from all over the world, and the concept is basically, "If you had power, absolute power, would you use it?" It focuses on a multicultural group of people from all over the world brought to the Midwest to be trained as warriors. Their main goal is to protect a cursed dagger from falling into the wrong hands. The project is a very important part of me because it's a fantastical story this is indirectly about my life. I've always seen myself as a film producer, but I wanted to do films that meant something, that had heart. That is what I am trying to do in Minnesota.

In spirit, I've always been an entrepreneur. However, I did work many mainstream jobs utilizing my skills. Everything from gymnastics to boxing, breakdancing, and, of course, martial arts. Eventually, I was able to work for myself. My first inspiration was my big brother Jose Fransico Figueroa (Frankie). He was the first in our family to attend college, and he truly supports my life in the field I've chosen.

I hope to bring Minnesota some interesting art, art that is very multicultural and very diversified. Minnesota is very Caucasian, and as a person of color who comes from a different country, I think that the art of movies and the context of stories can help Minnesotans learn a little bit more about different cultures. Even though it's an action film, I do try to shed light on the cultures that people come from. I hope Minnesota will open its doors, from an arts perspective, and embrace that art. That would be my ultimate goal. Hopefully people enjoy the kind of work I am trying to produce.

MEDIA LINKS

greencardvoices.org/speakers/jose-figueroa

Afterword

Immigrant entrepreneurs so clearly contribute to the US in a multitude of ways: inspiring innovation, creating new jobs, connecting the country to world markets, bringing different cultural perspectives to economic development, and countless others.

After the publication of this book, we plan to increase these stories' impact and amplify their tellers' voices by creating engaging programming that continues to break stereotypes and increase knowledge of the immigrant entrepreneurial experience. This programming includes a traveling multimedia exhibit featuring portraits, quotes, bios, and links to the storytellers' video narratives; a speaker series in which the immigrant entrepreneurs share their expertise in person; and a podcast series that focuses on the how-to aspect of each entrepreneur's story.

Immigration plays a significant role in the US; one in five Americans speak a language other than English at home. From boardrooms to book clubs, from MBA programs to "How to Start Your Own Business" workshops, from the business owner looking to understand her business partners to the individual interested in learning more about his immigrant neighbors, this book is an important resource for all Americans. We hope to spark deeply meaningful conversations about identity and our shared human experience while learning lessons about entrepreneurship that can benefit us all.

If you would like to learn more about speaking events, traveling exhibits, online videos, and other ways to engage with the *Green Card Entrepreneur Voices* stories, visit greencardvoices.org/entrepreneur-mn.

Glossary

AFS: a nonprofit that offers intercultural learning experiences through study abroad, language learning, gap year, volunteer, and host family programs.

Ayurveda: the traditional Hindu system of medicine, which is based on the idea of balance in bodily systems and uses dietary restrictions, herbal treatment, and yogic breathing.

curandera: a healer who uses folk remedies (in Spain and Latin America).

ERP (Enterprise Resource Planning) software: process management software that allows an organization to use a system of integrated applications to manage business and automate functions.

Giscard and Chirac: the French president and prime minister in 1974.

gofer: a person who runs errands, especially on a movie set or in an office.

green card: Also known as a Lawful Permanent Resident Card, an identification card attesting to the permanent resident status of an immigrant in the United States. The green card serves as proof that its holder, a Lawful Permanent Resident (LPR), has been officially granted immigration benefits, which include permission to reside and take employment in the United States. Green card also refers to an immigration process of becoming a permanent resident.

H1B: a nonimmigrant visa that allows US companies to employ graduate-level workers in occupations that require theoretical or technical expertise, in specialized fields such as IT, finance, accounting, architecture, engineering, mathematics, science, and medicine.

Jamaican patois: an English-based Creole language with West African influences spoken primarily in Jamaica and the Jamaican diaspora.

Jibaros: a Puerto Rican term used to refer to mountain people, who live in the heart of the island.

Khmer Rouge: the name given to Cambodian (Khmer) communists, and later the followers of the Communist Party of Kampuchea in Cambodia, who carried out the Cambodian genocide.

Khomeini: Iranian Shia Muslim religious leader and politician.

Madrasa: the Arabic word for any type of educational institution, whether secular or religious.

Maharishi Mahesh Yogi: a spiritual leader known for developing the Transcendental Meditation technique and spreading it all over the world.

Mexica: indigenous people of Mexico, colloquially known as the Aztecs.

naturalization: the process by which US citizenship is granted to a foreign citizen or national after he or she fulfills the requirements established by Congress in the Immigration and Nationality Act.

Quit India Movement: an Indian civil disobedience movement launched in August 1942, in response to Mahatma Gandhi's call for the immediate independence of India.

Red Stripe: a Jamaican beer.

re-education camps: name given to the prison camps operated by the communist government of Vietnam following the end of the Vietnam War.

refugee: a person outside their country of residence or nationality who is unable or unwilling to return and unable or unwilling to avail herself or himself of the protection of their original country of residence or nationality because of persecution or a well-founded fear of persecution on account of race, religion, nationality, membership in a particular social group, or political opinion.

resident/permanent resident: see "green card."

Sandinistas: a left-wing Nicaraguan political organization.

Santeria: pantheistic Afro-Cuban religious belief system developed from the beliefs and customs of the Yoruba people and incorporating some elements of the Catholic religion.

the Shah: a title for the former monarch of Iran, who was installed after a US-backed coup against the democratically elected government.

Somoza dictatorship: an influential political dynasty who ruled Nicaragua as a family from 1936–1979.

Standing Rock: Indian Reservation located in North Dakota and South Dakota, recently known as the location for a indigenous-led protest against the Dakota Access Pipeline.

StrengthsFinder: Web-based assessment of personality traits from the perspective of Positive Psychology.

Taíno: one of the indigenous peoples of the Caribbean.

Toastmasters: an international organization whose regional clubs support a positive learning experience; members are empowered to develop communication and leadership skills, resulting in greater self-confidence and personal growth.

Transcendental Meditation: a technique for detaching oneself from anxiety and promoting harmony and self-realization by meditation, repetition of a mantra, and other yogic practices, promulgated primarily by Maharishi Mahesh Yogi.

Trigueño/a: term used in Puerto Rico to describe someone whose skin color is between dark and light.

visa: a physical stamp in a passport or a document granted by a US embassy or consulate outside the US that permits the recipient to approach the US border and request permission to enter in a particular immigrant or nonimmigrant status.

About the Green Card Voices Team

Tea Rozman Clark, PhD is the Executive Director of Green Card Voices. She is an NYU graduate in Near and Middle Eastern studies and has a PhD in Cultural History, specializing in oral history recording from the University of Nova Gorica. She is first generation immigrant from Slovenia and 2015 Bush Leadership Fellow.

Rachel Mueller is the Program Manager at Green Card Voices. She is a graduate of Macalester College where she studied Anthropology and African Studies. She attended Waterford Kamhlaba United World College of Southern Africa in Swaziland where she lived for two years.

José Guzmán is the Lead Graphic Designer and Video Editor at Green Card Voices. After working with GCV as an intern in the summer of 2013, he remained with the team. He graduated from St. Olaf College in 2014 where he earned a BA in Studio Art.

Zamzam Ahmed is the Program Associate at Green Card Voices. She graduated from St. Catherine University with a degree in Political Science and International Relations. She is an immigrant from Somalia but was raised in Nairobi, Kenya and she entered the United States at the age of 8.

Raghu Aggarwal was invited to work on *Green Card Entrepreneur Voices* as an assistant editor. He was born in New Delhi, India and came to St. Paul, Minnesota to attend Macalester College where he studied International Studies and Public Health.

About Green Card Voices

Founded in 2013, Green Card Voices (GCV) is a nonprofit organization that utilizes storytelling to share personal narratives of America's immigrants, establishing a better understanding between the immigrant and nonimmigrant population. Our dynamic, video-based platform, book collections, and traveling exhibits are designed to empower a variety of educational institutions, community groups, and individuals to acquire first-person perspectives about immigrants' lives, increasing the appreciation of the immigrant experience in America.

Green Card Voices was born from the idea that the broad narrative of current immigrants should be communicated in a way that is true to each immigrant's story. We seek to be a new lens for those in the immigration dialogue and build a bridge between immigrants and nonimmigrants—newcomers and the receiving community—from across the country. We do this by sharing the firsthand immigration stories of foreign-born Americans, by helping others to see the "wave of immigrants" as individuals, with interesting stories of family, hard work, and cultural diversity.

To date, the Green Card Voices team has recorded the life stories of over three hundred immigrants coming from more than one hundred different countries. All immigrants that decide to share their story with GCV are asked six open-ended questions. In addition, they are asked to share personal photos of their life in their country of birth and in the US. The video narratives are edited down to five-minute videos filled with personal photographs, an intro, an outro, captions, and background music. These video stories are available on www.greencardvoices.org, and YouTube (free of charge and advertising).

Contact information:
Green Card Voices
2854 Columbus Ave South
Minneapolis, MN 55407

www.greencardvoices.org
612.889.7635

Facebook: www.facebook.com/GreenCardVoices
Twitter: www.twitter.com/GreenCardVoices

Immigrant Traveling Exhibits

The stories of each author of *Green Card Entrepreneur Voices* are featured in traveling exhibits, available to schools, universities, libraries, workplaces, and other venues where communities gather. Each exhibit features twenty stories from a particular city or with a particular theme, each with a portrait, a 200-word biography, and a quote from each immigrant. A QR code is displayed next to each portrait and can be scanned with a mobile device to watch the digital stories. The following programming can be provided with the exhibit: panel discussions, presentations, and community-building events.

Green Card Voices currently has seven exhibits based on different communities across the Midwest and South. To rent an exhibit, please contact us at 612.889.7635 or info@greencardvoices.com.

Now available:

Green Card Youth Voices:
Immigration Stories from a Minneapolis High School

The first book in the Green Card Youth Voices series, *Green Card Youth Voices: Immigration Stories from a Minneapolis High School* is a unique book of personal essays written by students from Wellstone International High School. Coming from 13 different countries, these young people share stories of family, school, change, and dreams. The broad range of experiences and the honesty with which these young people tell their stories is captured here with inspiring clarity. Available as an ebook (ISBN: 978-0-9974960-1-7) and paperback (ISBN : 978-0-9974960-0-0).

Contents:
- Full color portraits
- 30 personal essays by students from around the world
- Links to digital video stories on the Green Card Voices website
- Foreword by Kao Kalia Yang, award-winning author of *The Latehomecomer* and *The Song Poet*
- Excerpt from *Act4Change: A Green Card Voices Study Guide*
- Glossary

2016 Moonbeam Children's Gold Medal for Multicultural Non-Fiction Chapter Book

Foreword INDIES Finalist for Young Adult Nonfiction

Independent Press Awards winner for Best Young Adult Nonfiction

To purchase online and view a list of retailers, visit greencardvoices.org/books.

Also available on Amazon.

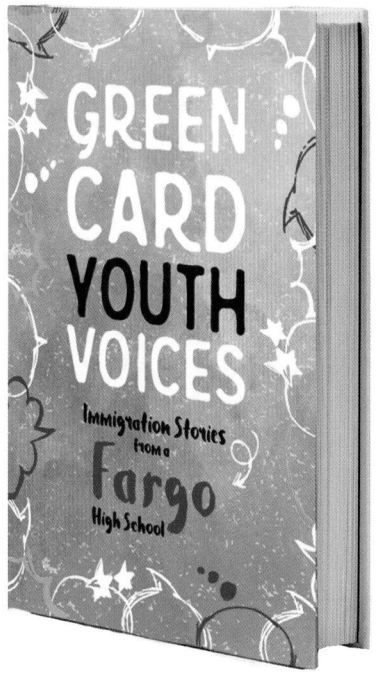

Also available:
Green Card Youth Voices:
Immigration Stories from a St. Paul High School

Based on the successful model used in Minneapolis, MN and Fargo, ND, *Green Card Youth Voices: Immigration Stories from a St. Paul High School* features 30 student authors from LEAP High School and is a vehicle to generate awareness about the immigrant experience. The book includes links to the students' video narrative, a study guide, and glossary to help teachers use the book as an educational resource when teaching about immigration. Available as an ebook (ISBN: 978-0-9974960-5-5) and paperback (ISBN : 978-0-9974960-3-1).

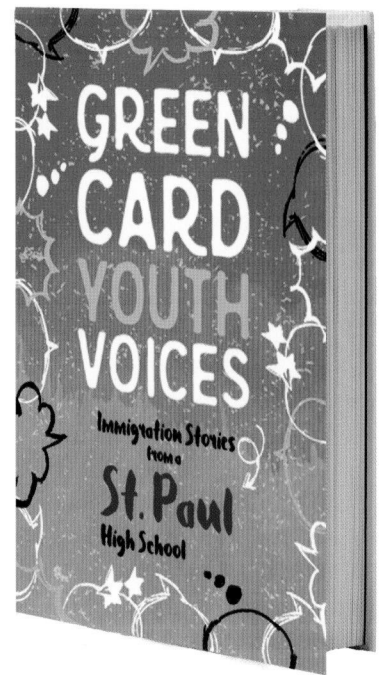

Midwest Book Awards Finalist
for Young Adult Nonfiction

Contents:

- Full color portraits
- 30 personal essays by students from around the world
- Links to digital video stories on the Green Card Voices website
- Excerpt from *Act4Change: A Green Card Voices Study Guide*
- Glossary

To purchase online and view a list of retailers,
visit greencardvoices.org/books.

Also available on Amazon.

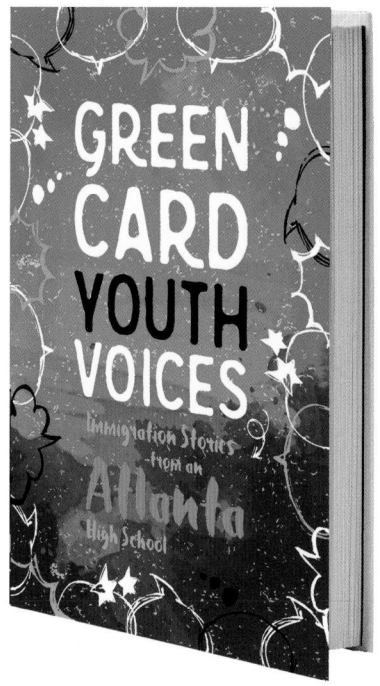